Typical Male
Syndrome

by Scott Henderson

Books

IA 15238

The contents of this work including, but not limited to, the accuracy of events, people, and places depicted; opinions expressed; permission to use previously published materials included; and any advice given or actions advocated are solely the responsibility of the author, who assumes all liability for said work and indemnifies the publisher against any claims stemming from publication of the work.

All Rights Reserved
Copyright © 2022 by Scott Henderson

No part of this book may be reproduced or transmitted, downloaded, distributed, reverse engineered, or stored in or introduced into any information storage and retrieval system, in any form or by any means, including photocopying and recording, whether electronic or mechanical, now known or hereinafter invented without permission in writing from the publisher.

RoseDog Books
585 Alpha Drive, Suite 103
Pittsburgh, PA 15238

Visit our website at *www.rosedogbookstore.com*

ISBN: 978-1-63867-455-9
eISBN: 978-1-63867-552-5

Typical Male Syndrome

Foreword:

I began this book many years ago when I was a young man and everything I thought I knew was suddenly wrong or irrelevant. Looking back, I could see the silliness of many of my actions and the sheer joy of living it day to day. That joy was something I hoped to pass along, and the idea of Typical Male Syndrome was born. For parents, and really everyone who enjoys the male/female dynamic, a good laugh or even just a smile is an important thing, for what we think, we become. The advice for this comes from God in Philippians 4:8: "Finally, brethren, whatever things are true, whatever things are noble, whatever things are just, whatever things are pure, whatever things are lovely, whatever things are of good report, if there is any virtue and if there is anything praiseworthy—meditate on these things."

    Scott Henderson

Typical Male Syndrome

Why does your little boy insist on testing an electric fence by peeing on it? Why does your college-age son have a competition rocket under his bed during a bomb squad search? Why does a man wait eight years to marry the perfect woman? Despite no medical support or government funding, I discovered the psychological driver behind these types of actions is an ancient malady, and unfortunately, it is widespread and hits close to home. Your husband has it; your boyfriend has it; and even your tiny newborn son has it. This terrible disease has no known cure nor cause. It afflicts approximately one half of the world's population, causing great suffering to its victims. It is a disease that haunts our planet and costs our families unknown money and time. Unknown, at least, until Mom can finally get Dad to stop the car so she can ask for directions or turn on the GPS. What is this horrible affliction? As its discoverer, I have officially named it Typical Male Syndrome, or TMS for short. Less enlightened members of my research family have called it Typical Male Stupidity, but this author prefers the proper scientific name. Other soon-to-be injured members have noted a similar name attributed to a certain female condition, but that observation is just plain crazy, and no sane (editor's note: chicken) male will mention it ever.

Now, what scientific credentials are needed to be an authority on TMS? Basically, none are required but the usual male conceit to sound confident when making things ups. Science and logic are lousy foils for hot air and baloney, which are the two driving forces of most male conversations. Still, this research is totally accurate and absolutely flawless in temperature and pork content. I admit, I started this research as a just another young, talented, charming, single male. Knowing nothing about the female species, I postulated that surely an insidious disease was creating a chemical blocker in the beta receptors of my brain. Some female non-scientists suggested other theories involving cluelessness, but they were surely flawed in their analyses. The evidence of a disease was overwhelming. What else could cause a male to get lost—on the way to his first date? Or cause one to break his nose before a homecoming kiss witnessed by his entire school? The research later took a very strange turn. I met and married a wonderful lady, and suddenly, symptoms changed. That athletic, talented, and charming young man was now described as a goofy husband and geeky father by multiple sources. Additionally, other athletic, talented, and charming young men around the main subject were also getting married…and being described similarly by multiple sources, which were observed as somewhat female in nature and totally smug in character. An epidemic seemed to have started that required more data. As the years of research/procrastination went by, more data (and more children) were gathered. With three kids and one unborn child that the good Lord now has, it was time to publish the results, both to provide a warning for posterity and to provide colleges with their required tuition. One conclusion is evident and must be addressed upfront. The female is the stronger and wiser of the human genders. To compensate this gross inequity of nature, biology evolved TMS to infect males with an innate ability to drive females of close proximity to insanity. Some may hypothesize that it is also a catch-all excuse for every dumb thing males do, but that is unsupported by exothermic reactions and pork content.

Typical Male Syndrome seems to infect only the male population, but the female population suffers the most from it; however, most fatalities are to the male carrier. One TMS researcher died quite suddenly after suggesting that TMS is actually caused by females. The poor man's research abruptly ended after a high heel was misplaced into his frontal lobe and the culprit managed to evade capture after a brief and uninspired investigation. Since this researcher is no dummy and fairly fond of keeping his brain intact, I focused my work only on symptoms. TMS begins at birth. Male babies are messier than females, often peeing several feet into the air to the adoring cheers of their dads and disgruntled amusement of the nurses who have the unfortunate job of cleaning the display. This seems to condition the young males via affirmation principles to practice and perfect such actions, advancing the theory that TMS has a psychological element to its intensity, thus resulting in the symptom further developing into adulthood as evidenced by the inhumane state most men's restrooms maintain. Regrettably, other worldly influences are in effect at this early stage as well. All over the maternity ward, male babies are being told how handsome they are, how smart, etc. Yet, they share a striking resemblance with Shar Pei dogs and act like evil gnomes, howling like unsettled spirits after a slight hunger pain. Being subject to the sounds as close observers, female babies quickly learn about the pains of childbirth and can associate such to the presence of males. Truthfully, however, those first few moments in the hospital also allow for a time of beauty as this is the time that a new dad begins to feel the responsibilities and privilege that are attributed with fatherhood. TMS is suspended and he speaks little, simply honored to be able to witness the miraculous and blessed scene of a mother holding his newborn child.

Immediately after birth, a male child will continue to show signs of TMS in subtle but messy ways. In fact, TMS tends to only strengthen over time. Male children instinctively begin comparing themselves to their peers in what some would call unorthodox manners. Yes, they still see who can pee the farthest distance and usually test their prowess in the most public areas. Any time when Mom and Dad seemed distracted, young boys often aim at the nearest busy road and let it fly (with Dad silently approving). Clothes are also always good indicators of TMS, as clothing seems rather optional for boys. This especially comes out around visitors, including the local pastor's wife, to the dismay of Mom. Furthermore, all the normal items of a fashion ensemble are not always included in the young male's attire of the day. Underwear may be forgotten, even on baseball practice days when the featured drill is sliding through dirt and rocks into bases. Even when clothing is used, it may be worn in unforeseen ways. Shirts are often worn over the head, especially when running. Collisions are inevitable when this happens, with the only lesson learned being that running when blind can hurt. Travel also brings out TMS, usually exhibited by high velocity projectile vomiting due to motion sickness. When a young male enters this particular stage, he is a virtual volcano, and usually the explosive, high altitude kind. Fortunately, truck stops are full of very powerful and strange-smelling cleaners. Our van once made a twenty-two-hour trip to Florida with a powerful orange smell despite the fact we were not carrying any oranges. Truck stops are also full of ornery truckers and mean-looking bikers, also strange smelling, but never fear these characters when dealing with clean-ups because even these tough guys shrink back in fear of chemical warfare. A cute, dainty mom or hilariously nerdy dad has a clear path through the toughest truck stop while carrying a towel-full of junior's breakfast. On a personal note, I think I once stopped a biker gang war while so armed.

The early years of TMS do not begin to prepare one for the teenage years, because the disease really kicks in with the onset of puberty. The frequency and intensity of these attacks also seems directly proportional to proximity of young females. To the amateur observer, a very shallow analysis of the habits of a young single male would seem to revolve around impressing as many young females as possible. Fortunately for the amateur observer, a shallow analysis covers the subject just fine. A young TMS-infected male will try all sorts of actions and impersonations to impress young females, but being a success with women is really very simple—he just needs to be himself. This always works as long as the subject is handsome, charming, rich, and not very smart. If he is not, the young male will need to know a few things about the opposite gender. This brings out a vocabulary obstacle involving an alternative to the word gender. A young male should never, ever say the "s" word, as in the word "~~sex~~." Saying such a provocative word would immediately cause an onset of TMS symptoms such as embarrassing giggles and pimples to the young, naive male. Because his ignorance can get him eaten or engaged, the TMS-infected youth should be educated about women as soon as he practically can. Unfortunately, by then he is probably a grandfather.

TMS and Places to Meet

Females are far superior to males (period) and are especially superior at knowing where to meet potential mates. This is the reason you see so many young females working at hardware stores, going to church, graduating at universities, etc. These females are looking for strong, smart, handy, and nice young males. This is, of course, like hunting the mythological unicorn. Churches seem logical since the messages should center on love and mercy and the females wistfully theorize the males might actually understand a word or two. As for mercy, that is for the females to have on their male projects. At the very least, the young females will have the legendary church ladies around to guide them toward more acceptable and trainable young males. These ladies can also frighten the young males into obedient submission. Universities are places of higher learning for females and locations for males to theoretically advance in their knowledge and wisdom and possibly grow into respectable adults. Since universities are expensive and require some degree of intelligence and discipline to attend, the females at least get the see the relatively book smarter and financially resourceful males. Unfortunately, too many male subjects only research the economics of beer pricing and the physics of keg balancing. The serious ones are stuck in male-dominated majors such as engineering where they are hard to find because they are hidden away in forgotten corners of the college library or musty laboratories, building the aforementioned competition rockets later discovered under their dorm room beds by the local SWAT team while responding to a fake bomb threat call (no arrests made). Because of minor difficulties like intoxication, handcuffs, and potential explosions, the rational thought process of females in finding suitable males at universities can be thwarted. Looking for acceptable males in hardware stores is a strangely haunted hunt. Because most young males coming into the stores are usually there in support of some family project, they most likely are helping out at home. Thus, these young men are considered trustworthy, hardworking, and kind. The young females' theories are not always correct, but their logic would make Freud proud. Unfortunately, these males may be oblivious (a common male trait) due to being possessed by the evil spirit of Home Improvement who prevents them from noticing all things organic which a human female most certainly is. Online dating services are also intelligent resources for meeting prospective dates and mates. These services use logic, common interests, similar beliefs, and other personal attributes to match up suitable couples. This would seem to be foolproof, except that with males, that is an oxymoron. Highly intelligent, male computer scientists will not be able to turn on the program. Teachers and English majors will not be able to write out the descriptions. Only those who can randomly hit the right keys can actually input the correct data. Of course, any female can handle it easily enough, though they fret they are not using just the right words in their detailed biographies, wondering if "sophisticated" means "snobby," "serious" means "desperate," or "enjoys going out" means "high-maintenance." While they worry, the males crash the database. Despite all of these obstacles, females still must be considered the best at looking for suitable males, whose efforts are simply pathetic.

Males are clearly not that smart at working where the type of girls they claim to desire actually visit. Most young males are looking for beautiful fashion models, but these types of women rarely work lawn maintenance and construction jobs which seem to attract young males. These women rarely lay asphalt in 110-degree heat nor do they get hourglass figures by pigging out at fast food restaurants. Logically, if a young male wanted to meet a beautiful female, he should work in a lingerie store like Victoria's Secrets. However, no young male would even go near such a store. Young males are known for their coarse bragging when it comes to their alleged experience with women, but nothing silences their bravado like their attempts to stay cool when walking past such a store in the mall. Even the crudest males will cross over to the opposite side of the aisle to avoid such a place. If they happen to accidentally bump into a female while crossing over, even an entire wrestling team would blush. Yet, a lingerie store is just the right place to meet beautiful models and also avoid all other males. Perhaps the latter is *why* females shop there. This is not to say that wonderful young females do not work construction and lawn maintenance. Many do, exhibiting strength and dedication, two traits of excellent mates. The difficulty for males simply centers on their inability to notice these important characteristics. Fortunately for the females, there are often tools and construction materials around to beat some sense in the young males if/when necessary.

Suspicious females may wonder how I know about such stores as Victoria's Secrets. Yes, I have been in such stores while searching for my wife, and I was quite embarrassed as I entered, but I loved my wife and I wanted to find her, so I was willing to sacrifice my pride. I had seen her deliver my children with perfect strangers watching so I figured I could do this. I was actually not all that embarrassed. After all, who could be embarrassed about things you did not understand? I knew I was looking at clothing, but I could not comprehend where it would go on the female anatomy. Since the stuff could all be scarves for the head for all I knew, I was not flustered. My grandmother wore scarves and I did not blush when I saw her. Fortunately, I found my wife before I had time to consider the relationship between Victoria's Secrets clothing and my grandmother.

Teenage TMS and the Cardinal Rules of Female Warfare

Throughout history, many brilliant men have written about the cardinal rules of warfare, Clausewitz, Mahan, etc. Most have written about such things in order that the nations' rulers and military leaders might be taught enough about fighting that they could keep their heads. For young males with TMS, they need to know a few rules about dealing with females if they want to keep their noggins on as well.

Rule 1: Know thy enemy. First of all, women are not the enemy. This is fortunate because no male knows anything about women and never will. If one claims he knows something, he is either a liar or a hopelessly outwitted husband. Fortunately for us, women do not know a thing about men either. This is the primary reason there will never be a war of the sexes, because they both see each other as a totally different and incomprehensible species. How we can come together and produce children has got to be nature's greatest mystery. Knowing that males and females really do not know each other and that they follow this basic rule of warfare has surely prevented the extermination of all humans. To prepare for the possibility of conflict with females, males do regularly train, usually by golfing and fishing. These sports allow males to strategize with equally clueless buddies while participating in activities that defy all logic, a practice that prepares them for first dates and long-lasting marriages. Males also use these exercises as training for subterfuge and propaganda, because males also lie about women, golf, and fishing in about equal amounts.

Since women are not the enemy, who is? The answer for the young males is themselves and their hormones. What man can resist a pretty face? Even infant boys gurgle and squeal at the sight of their mothers. Grandfathers can still react to that look in his wife's eyes, even if it is caused by dirty bifocals. Intelligence does not matter against the internal enemy. The smartest man in the world is a brainless fool near a pretty woman. All females possess this power over men starting at birth. This can be seen at a maternity ward. Pound for pound, the most powerful person in the world is a female infant. She can twist a two-hundred-pound father around her tiniest finger with minimal effort. In my personal case, the squeeze was certainly worth it.

Rule 2: Avoid needless talk. Speaking with a woman should be avoided when possible to prevent offense. Notice that couples are not asked to speak much during marriage ceremonies. This is to avoid embarrassments at the altar. All the couples must do is repeat things and say a lot of "I wills" and "I dos." The reason speaking is so dangerous is because males simply do not understand that certain words and phrases can trigger PDST (pretty darn serious trouble) when overheard by females. The S-word is a good example. Say sex to even the most amorous woman and you will be slapped or even worse, given the cold shoulder. Talking about children is usually a good subject except when around your bratty little relatives, which will trigger an early end to a male's hope of a second date. Pregnancy is also a very bad subject, especially in the last two months of one. The idea that all women are especially beautiful when they are pregnant (which is actually true) was started by a husband in deep tribulation with his wife. In fact, a pregnant wife is scarier than a praying mantis, and the husband knows very well how that ends up. When expecting, even innocent subjects like sports can lead to male distress. The average woman can somehow misconstrue deep sports team dedication and come up with the conclusion "You care more about that stupid team than me!" This is especially troublesome when an important game causes the male to forget an anniversary or a doctor's appointment. One way to avoid this is to marry outside the regular playing season to a girl born outside the regular playing season. Another wise guy idea is to marry a girl on his own birthday so he can always seem excited about its approach. An absolutely brilliant maneuver is to marry on his birthday to a girl who was born on his birthday, especially in the off-season.

Even when pregnancy is not an issue, the weather is not a good subject either. If a male says it is going to storm, a female will think he is trying to scare her. If he remarks about a full moon, she will conclude he is trying to seduce her. If he says the weather is nice, then she thinks he wants to golf or go fishing and can instantly lead to comments like, "You like nice weather so you can get away from me!" Immediate denials are called for in this case, especially if the male never seems to actually catch fish. Sorrowful tears would also help as long as they are not shed due to the sliced drives and the lack of fish. Other subjects are bad, too. If he talks about dogs, she will like cats. If he talks about cats, she will be allergic to them or, logically, think he is weird and talks to them. Talk about fashion will reveal his incredibly bad taste and may indicate, to her, that he is just interested in looks anyway. As this researcher has discovered (please do not ask how), there really are no safe subjects for males to discuss around females; however, as my young female offspring remarked after reading this paragraph, "It's not exactly as if the world is lacking without the male input."

Another reason why a young male should avoid talking is that he cannot actually speak coherently to a female. The typical single male's first response to a pretty girl is to gag, grunt, or fart, often at the same time. If he manages to say something, he spits on her blouse before the third word is spoken. The first sentence will definitely contain grammatical and logistic errors such as "The team football team sure footballed good today," or "The band was really, uh, band tonight." Intelligence has no bearing on the degree of incompetence in the first encounter. In fact, the higher the man is on the evolutionary scale, the more he will sound like a baboon. Even memory is affected when a male is around a female. Some male nuclear physicists have undergone verbal meltdown and have simply forgotten to breathe. Men who know the date and time their team won the John Deere Plow and Associated Implements Bowl cannot remember their own anniversaries, the time of their dates, etc. The poor guy just meeting a girl will not be able to follow directions to his own home, even less likely instructions to her home. As a helpful reminder, the male should always have the girl meet somewhere in public for the first date. She will feel less threatened, and the guy can find out where the place is later with the help of an app map and his mother. A young male simply does not realize females' favorite (and the overall safest) topic of conversation is about the males in their lives. The single females talk about how great their boyfriends are. A female research subject who had just been in a fight with her boyfriend casually declared, "If we get over this, we will probably get married." Based on these probabilities, this couple did marry and must have had several more conflicts because they now have about half a dozen children. This brings us to the strange fact that females find their charming and intelligent boyfriends suddenly becoming boring and dumb after matrimony, a finding, which if investigated, would likely be proven true both in the present and past. So even if the young male is making progress at speaking to his girlfriend, after marriage he will have to learn a new language, likely another strange and foreign tongue.

To make options worse, silence for a young male is very bad, at least as a first impression. A quiet guy is assumed to be conceited, passive, shy, grumpy, grouchy, or just plain weird. Some quiet guys are assumed to even be nice guys, which is the worst possible reputation to have while dating. One would think that two strangers just getting to know each other would expect some awkward moments of silence, but both typically assume silence means they are not right for each other. Actually, many people are quiet around those they are most interested in; they are just too shy to speak. When a couple can tolerate silence when together (and the female would surely appreciate the absence of an all-knowing and all-saying male), it means that they are comfortable with each other and where they stand with the other. However, silence works in the opposite way as well. If one member of a couple is quiet, the other may see them as cold and defensive. Silence can be a fortress or a prison.

Rule 3: Never mention a woman's age. Males should never try to guess a female's age. Once while talking with a couple I guessed to be in their fifties, the subject of age came up, and I cleverly underestimated the lady's age by about fifteen years. Her husband, by the way, was a law officer who was carrying a gun and casually mentioned that he had gotten into some civil rights trouble. My guess was low by only four years, and my near-miss with death left me shaking in my sneakers. Another problem arises if the male is right, because few women are satisfied with their ages. There are some scientific guidelines that may keep a young male reasonably safe. If a female is not wearing diapers or does not mention her AARP membership, she is twenty-five, always and forever. This is the safest known age to mention for a female from age ten to seventy. If she blushes and says she is just sixteen, the young male should confess that he was intimidated by her sophistication and grace. Now, this is fine for impressing the local Sonic girl (who knows you might even get the right order) or even the football cheerleaders, but older females are not as easily impressed. Of course, they know the male is lying. I once heard a good line in an old Cary Grant movie about this situation. Cary, a great role model, was flattering an older lady in order to secure her good graces in pursuing a younger relative. That wise woman remarked something to the effect, "I am old enough to know better, but young enough to like it." After the age of seventy or so, females begin to fess up about their ages. At this time, they become proud of their longevity and their ability to endure and occasionally enjoy all the dumb things their husbands, sons, and even grandsons have done. They can also get quite ornery when you shortchange them. Fortunately, these little young-at-heart ladies are very forgiving. These ladies also are a great source of information, too. These ladies may have lots of granddaughters they will happily introduce to nice young males. They will also point out their granddaughters' pet peeves as helpful warnings. Be warned, though. They are totally ruthless to fakes and can spot them right away. They will eat such a foolish young male faster than the fearsome female praying mantis, and no one will mourn.

Rule 4: Avoid certain subjects. This rule is an expansion of Rule 2. Most males have probably heard that the subject of sex is bad, but that is because young males cannot pronounce the word without snorting some liquid out their noses, mouths, ears, and southern parts. Religion and politics can be discussed; however, these subjects get males into losing intellectual contests with females who are intrinsically much smarter. There are some positives to these subjects, if the male is not too much of a sore loser. If the young male and his date can both argue, get mad, and still like each other later, this is very good. The male may even follow what the female is saying, and sometimes miracles happen and he may even agree with her. Overall, this is good marriage practice, because the phrase "You are right, dear" is considered a medical miracle against TMS and indicates to all nearby females that a considerate and intellectually advanced male is present, a truly rare and endangered species worthy of female protection. Subjects males should always avoid include pets, clothes, females in general, and ex-girlfriends in particular. Males and females cannot agree on pets, so this subject should be avoided like a minefield. The reason is simple: females like obnoxious pets and males like dumb, slobbery ones. Females tend to like cats because felines hate males. For instance, tigers are sometimes called man-eaters but never female-eaters. Males tend to like dogs, especially ones that roll in mud and are not housebroken, thus making their owners look better in comparison. Another subject to avoid is clothing. Males do not understand color coordination nor style. This goes for their clothing, women's clothing, baby clothing, etc. Why Garanimals, which features animal types to help kids come up with matching clothes based on animal labels, has not come up with a men's clothing and shoe line is beyond marketing comprehension. Naturally, a female always asks a male what he thinks of something she is wearing. Of course, he foolishly fails to run away and just stands there and states his opinion despite lack of knowledge or common sense. This opinion is always wrong, period. The female involved pretends to get mad, and the male is left wondering what happened. In nature, this is comparable to a cat playing with a mouse before eating it, a characteristic that also explains why females like cats. Another subject to avoid is relationships. Females actually like this word because they can twist it to mean what they want. A single male thinks a relationship with a female means he is related to them. A female interprets it differently. If she likes the male, their relationship is a precursor to marriage. If she does not particularly care about the male, their relationship is the dreaded "just friends" type. Most males know the "just friends" statement means she wants you to nicely drop dead. Since the term "relationship" can mean anything the female wants, the male should best leave the word unspoken.

Rule 5: Surrender when outnumbered. When outnumbered, the wise male should surrender. Of course, one male with one female is hopelessly outnumbered, so surrender is a good option in all situations. However, when literally outnumbered, the male should say nothing. In a crowd of females, the lone male sacrifice should never get in a discussion with even one, because they will all join in against him. The situation is like what happens when a male wildebeest is attacked by a pride of hungry lionesses, only messier. If asked to state an opinion, the male should smile stupidly and say, "I don't know." The females will laugh, but this is safe. When they laugh, the would-be male victim should laugh a little, too. This indicates an understanding of the subject and a sense of self-depreciation. Of course, escape is always the best option. If the group is moving, just lag behind and the pack will forget about their scared victim. If trapped in a room, the bathroom excuse is always good, especially if it is in another state. The important thing, though, is for the male to just get away.

TMS and Courtship

Females seem to know instinctively how to attract males and never seem to do or say anything wrong. They can approach guys in subtle, yet safe ways, i.e., in a group. This is called the Pack Attack approach. They can flirt around and find out if a guy is interested in them without revealing that they are interested in him. This is a smart and mature way of dating. Males, though, bomb at anything subtle. They rarely pick up hints from girlfriends and often miss outright commands from wives. They tend to approach would-be girlfriends about like the Germans approached things in World War II. Historians called the German attacks blitzkrieg. Males call it asking a girl out. This technique has been analyzed extensively, simply because this method failed in war and males love to study losers because it makes them feel better. This explains the fascination with the male praying mantis. Evidence thoroughly indicates (okay, I guessed) that males just do not have the gumption to stay cool in the presence of a female for more than a few moments. After five minutes near a cute girl, a boy's courage fades and he simply must run for cover. If he refuses to run, he becomes paralyzed with fear and starts to hyperventilate. His oxygen-starved brain now cannot control his mouth, which usually begins uttering inane words and phrases. Hopefully, the young girl has accepted his request for a date and he has already gotten such pertinent information like her address. His confused mutterings then leave the girl wondering if maybe the date was not such a good idea, but with time and additional oxygen, the guy usually survives long enough to make the date and thus make a fool out of himself all over again.

Now suppose a TMS-infected male somehow survives an introduction and gets an actual date with a live female. The first thing he should remember is where he is supposed to meet the girl, bearing in mind as stated before his memory is affected by TMS. If it is at her home, he should get the address, in writing and in multiple electronic formats, backed up in a reliable database secured with a simple password like "password." Directions might even help, but should be referenced from the nearest sports stadium. GPS and other electronic means are very efficient and will give verbal instructions to the user. Unfortunately, many of these devices use female voices which the male will likely misunderstand. A female voice that says turn right will somehow mean vote republican and go straight. Turn left will ensure a democratic vote and a vehicle sent into reverse. These electronic devices can also produce male voices which the male can actually hear, but he will argue with this male voice because no electronic male can ever be right. There is a natural law at work here that explains the reluctance to follow directions. Males somehow made many scientific discoveries and advances, often after causing some calamity (note the tale of Ben Franklin being credited with discovering electricity after flying a kite in a lightning storm), but they have never written a useable users' manual despite repeating the inane instructions in multiple languages. Software, toys, and general mechanical equipment are primes examples of these shortcomings. Based on these manuals, sports cars have been converted to lawnmowers; toys have been turned into lethal weapons which the male eventually liked after the hospital stay; and software has crashed so much that Big Chief tablet sales are skyrocketing. With this history, an electronic male voice is thus heard with valid skepticism. Therefore, finding a first date is truly a worthy and dangerous search and rescue mission. The danger of having to call up a date an hour late and ask for directions is very real and I will not disclose how I know this. Blind dates tend to eliminate some of the dangers to the male. If the male forgets where he is supposed to meet and loses her phone number, he will be afraid she is angry with him (for once a logical conclusion), but she will analyze herself and wonder what she did wrong. She will never figure out that the male was just plain dumb. Blind dates, like electronic dating services, are sort of logical, which is why males generally do not feel comfortable with them. If the arrangers of the blind date know the couple well, they can really set up very compatible people. Of course, most males often fall for those hopelessly out of their league, which does limit the selection and often frustrates the would-be matchmaker. It thus takes cunning and persistence to pull this off. It is folly to think of a successful matchmaker as a Cupid, though. Cupid is a mythological figure. He is also a he. No male is capable of being setting up two people for romance, with fathers as the worst. They see sweet, smart, strong young ladies and want to set their sons up with them. Interestingly enough, this effort seems devoid of TMS symptoms because it is based on sound logic and reasonable observation. However, the son will not listen under any circumstances and would actually decline to be set up with a girl even if she were a supermodel if Dad was involved. Because matchmakers must be females, mothers, who are naturally gifted in such matters, are logical choices, but sons are nearly as resistant to them as to their fathers. The name of this resistance is called the Ick Factor for reasons that will not be detailed but purged forever. Female friends of the male involved are potential dates, so suggestions from them are considered mere diversions. Female cousins are definitely qualified, but the absolute best are sisters. Sisters know their brothers well, especially their weaknesses, which are many. My sister definitely knew mine. I am embarrassed but utterly happy to say my sister set me up with the best blind date I ever had. My date was my future bride, Jeannine. It was embarrassing in that it hurt my TMS-infected ego to admit that my sister, in plain country terms, found me a woman. The circumstances were, of course, catastrophic. In the fall of 1986, eastern Oklahoma was hit by some of the worst flooding in its history. My wife lived with her sister and brother-in-law in a flood-prone area below a lake controlled by the agency where my father and I worked. At the time, Jeannine worked with my sister but did not know anything about me. After her home was inundated with several feet of water, she was not happy with my agency. She expressed her feelings at her workplace in earshot of my sister, who somehow felt inspired to set us up. Looking back, I always claim that my sister harbored a deep grudge against Jeannine for her remarks, because at the first chance, my sister set Jeannine up with me. After three childbirths, I guess we taught her a thing or two about Henderson family revenge. In reality, my sister has always been a trooper to me. She is a beautiful, smart lady with a wonderful family and lucky husband. She has been a great source of advice for caring for our children, and she was a great comfort when we lost our first in a miscarriage. I have always been surrounded by strong women in my family and my sister is just one example. Since brothers are not allowed to publicly or privately praise their sister, you may assume that this paragraph was written by someone else.

Sometimes, despite all the warning signs of a bad infection of TMS, the dating starts to get serious. TMS reasserts itself in especially insidious ways as the relationship winds down toward marriage. It makes a male even move oblivious to the fact he is about to make one of the biggest and most life altering decisions of his life. This is what happily happened to me. As my wife and I got more serious about our relationsh—well, that thingy-a-bob word that must not be spoken by a male, I started to think about marriage. With all the confidence of a fish in a desert, I once predicted that "The way we are going, we are probably going to get married." I am sure Jeannine knew we were meant to be by this time and had known for several months, but I had not popped the question. That fateful summer, Jeannine went on her annual trip to Florida to visit her grandparents. During that trip, I received a postcard from her in which she wrote how she missed me and that she loved me. That did it for me. I figured a girl thoughtful enough to send me a postcard was awfully good wife material (and I was right on that account). Summoning all my courage, I decided to "propose" in the most non-committal way possible. The first night I saw her after she got back, we spent a relaxing evening eating and visiting with her father. We went outside in the moonlight and talked, and, well, we did kiss a little. Then I "proposed" by asking, "Why don't we go ring shopping?" I explained that I would not "officially" propose without a ring and without knowing that her answer would be yes. Immediately, she assured me the answer was the affirmative. Now I had counted on the ring shopping to take several weeks which would give my cold feet more time to thaw. In about two days, I was having an out-of-the-body experience in the jewelry shop writing out a large check for an engagement ring and two wedding rings. The stereotypical female is a careful and deliberate shopper, meaning slow to all males, but not when it comes to picking out rings. It took Jeannine about five minutes to pick out her two rings, in stock and on sale. After thirty minutes of indecision, I finally picked out my one ring. Later that same week, they were fitted and ready to go. I was still in a daze. But like a confused young bull calf that will blindly follow the old cow path, I was easily herded forward. And a sweeter ramrod could not be found! Later that week, with rings in hand and on one knee, I asked Jeannine to be my wife. The story still brings tears to my eyes and I thought I was being very romantic, but to this day, Jeannine laughs about my waiting to have the rings to officially propose. I insist that this is not only romantic, it is practical and sensible. The idea of a man spontaneously buying an engagement ring and suddenly springing it out makes no sense to me. First, what if she says, "No thanks." Do you think the jewelry shop will just happily refund you the money? Second, there is no way a male will know what size ring his intended wears. Undoubtedly, he will pick out a ring size that just about fits her biceps. Thirdly, an engagement ring is something that a woman would wear for the rest of her life. Would any sensible female trust a male's TMS-warped sense of alleged taste? To this day, I cannot describe my wife's ring in the proper jewelry terms, because "pretty" and "sparkly" apparently are not correct. Expensive is definitely not the right term. Well, that's my argument for being romantic, but being a male researcher on TMS, I know I am wrong. At least Jeannine credits me with being sentimental, just not romantic. Whatever that means.

TMS displays interesting symptoms around the time the male is preparing for the marriage ceremony, too. For instance, I was in a state of oblivion for months before my wedding. When we were planning for our wedding, I say "we" rather liberally for my own benefit as I was in a total fog, Jeannine must have known I was scared silly and had planned accordingly. While we were setting a date, my nerves were not prepared for a brief engagement period, and when I was saying I did not want to get married immediately, she was ready with her arguments against a year-long engagement. This was in July. I then told her I did not want to get married real soon, as in September. As visions of an unwanted year-long engagement melted under the panic of picking out wedding attire, punchbowls, and the like in just two months, she rather clearly made known her honest feelings by screaming, "September?!" We were both relieved to settle on November 5th without having any more panic attacks. During the time between the proposal and the actual wedding, I discovered TMS does have helpful aspects such as numbing the prospective groom. Numbness of the mouth is always a good thing for a male and is especially helpful to the soon-to-be groom who just does not comprehend the approaching storm/wedding. His intended (this term sort of sounds like a deer that a hunter just missed) does not get off so easily. She makes numerous plans and coordinates what seems like a million details. Her female relatives are often involved, both helping and irritating her. Again, TMS actually aids the male.

Typical Male Syndrome | 19

Since he has no clue as to what is happening, he never mentions anything about the wedding plans. She interprets his silence as strong support and understanding. The truth is, he has no idea what and who she is talking about. When she rants and raves about her mother's insistence on using Aunt Martha's service set, he silently wonders why she needs a tool set. Luckily for him, she changes the subject and is soon gushing about how helpful cousin Mary is in locating a garter. He now wonders why she needs a fishing guide for gars. Fortunately for both, the girl is so full of excitement that she does not stop talking long enough for the male to say anything stupid, which is a redundant statement because anything he would say would be stupid. He is cognizant enough to know that his beloved is happy and in the mood to hug and kiss a lot, so he remains content and clueless. Of course, he does occasionally wonder what kind of party his betrothed is planning.

With this November deadline, my wife had her work cut out for her. She also had to deal with her own sense of confusion about what was happening. Her first dose of reality came when she posed in her wedding dress for pictures. Now *she* realized she was really getting married. She expressed her emotions to me on this and I was sweetly understanding which meant that I just cluelessly hugged her. I also exhibited the TMS symptoms of oblivion to most things female when it came to the arrangements for the wedding. I had no opinions on anything, which is the perfect way to soothe the stressed bride-to-be. The few decisions she made me make, I did quickly, usually with her guidance and always in her presence. I handled our honeymoon arrangements with ESPECIALLY adroit skill; I called my aunt, the travel agent, and she did everything. TMS kept me fully insulated from reality until the rehearsal. After that trial run, I simply could not avoid the thought I was getting married for forever on the next day. That was when I figured out why couples repeated vows—they could never remember anything by themselves. I was a nervous wreck, but by the grace of God, I did not pass out at the wedding and Jeannine and I were married Nov 5, 1994. And I have a video to prove it.

During our engagement period, I was introduced to Jeannine's grandparents. We were the usual nervous couple, enjoying countless photo sessions and jokes. Her grandfather was really getting into the picture taking. He finally corralled Jeannine and me together and announced that this would be the final picture of us while we were still normal. Of course, we all laughed, but come to think of it, he was right. After marriage and children, we have not been normal since, unless normal means being on the run constantly, being forever tired, having a vocabulary that revolves around bowel movements, and being extremely happy. If this is not normal, I hope we are forever abnormal.

TMS and Pregnancy

Typical Male Syndrome is especially lethal during pregnancy. The expectant father is already likely to be excited, frightened, and thoroughly stressed out during this time and thus is an easy victim to an especially bad outbreak of the disease. One early sign that an attack is coming on is insomnia. This usually begins one night as the husband is about to drop off to sleep. His wonderful wife snuggles up next to him and utters those immortal words, "Honey, I think I'm pregnant," and then rolls over and goes to sleep. At this point, TMS kicks in, and all thoughts of sleep are gone. Instantly, the husband thinks of Lamaze classes, dirty diapers, and college tuition. The insomnia seems to last for about twenty-five years. Now, no one is sure how TMS causes insomnia. Some rather courageous male researchers have noted a correlation between the time of the pregnancy notification and the onset of insomnia, thus advancing the theory that TMS is activated by close proximity to females, but they mysteriously died before they finished their research. This researcher has not advanced this theory and is not about to start.

Pregnancy is a serious situation and cannot be taken lightly. It is literally a life-threatening condition for the unborn child and the mother, but it can also be a life-threatening time for the expectant father. My kind and gentle wife never threatened me with death more than when she was expecting. These threats seemed to occur most frequently during discussions of family size. When I would say I wanted twins or triplets, I was sure to be threatened, often to cheers from other female relatives. I never reported such threats because I figured a male police officer would not believe them and a female officer might supply Jeannine with a Taser. Nevertheless, I survived by my wits (or lack thereof) and my wife's realization that at least I would be a built-in diaper disposal. Other males, I am told, have not been so lucky. One unfortunate fellow, while witnessing the ultrasound of his triplets, was reported to have gleefully exclaimed, "Puppies!" The subsequent ultrasound of his brain revealed nothing but future trouble because it is a well-documented fact that a wife, like an elephant, never forgets. It is also recommended that any analogies with females and elephants be totally avoided when either are present or pregnant.

Pregnancy brings out the worst in TMS, especially to the region around the open mouth. A male cannot speak to a pregnant wife without producing dreadful results. Suppose the wife is concerned about her appearance. She is at that stage where she wonders if people realize she is pregnant and not just gaining a few extra pounds. The helpful husband then reassures her with the words, "Sugar, you are not showing, you are mass advertising!" This somehow does not come across well. Saying such things as "I know my wife is around here somewhere, she is around everywhere" is also not considered by hormone-driven females as being sensitive. Remarking that your wife looks radiant while pregnant seems to translate to the wife as, "Honey, I want to make love to you right now." This instantly produces revulsion hormones similar to those that cause morning sickness. The wife does not just say, "Not tonight, dear, I have a headache." No, her look instantly gives the terrified husband the headache instead. The fact that she translated the original statement correctly just gives insult to injury. A statement such as "I am so glad we are pregnant" produces terrible thoughts in a wife's mind. She hears this as "Thank goodness I cannot bear children." This instantly turns into a battle of the sexes involving the "what if males had all the babies" quip. Another thing not to say to a pregnant wife is "Sugar, you sure look healthy." This innocent statement translates to the wife as "You sure are fat." After she becomes very agitated, the husband will inevitably try to soothe his wife. He will say things like, "Dear, I did not mean to upset you, you know I love you." This translates as "Dear, you outweigh me by thirty pounds, please don't eat me." Remarking that this pregnancy will be the first of many is very, very bad. Juries consider such sentiments as proof of justifiable homicide. I said this often to my wife Jeannine during her pregnancy with our firstborn son Cole. I survived only by the foresight of my loving wife. She knew she would need some help raising this child, and I was the most convenient candidate. Granted, I did not have much potential as a mother, but a father can at least occupy space in a child's life. For instance, a father is a great target when a little baby boy does his thing without the benefit of a diaper. Plus, fathers have a greater appreciation of the physics of a baby. A mother would never exclaim about the incredible velocity and travel distance of a bowel movement, but fathers find such things fascinating, if not also deeply disturbing. Another subject to avoid speaking out loud is about how well your wife is handling her pregnancy. This translates to "Pregnancy is no big deal; women are such whiners about such a trivial medical condition." The wife then launches into a tirade about how easy the husband's role is and how awful he is to get her into such a horrible condition. The poor husband, who meant the statement as a compliment of her courage and endurance (and deep-seated gratitude that he was not having the baby), is, of course, startled when he gets hit with "the look." This attribute of women seems to react with TMS in a manner that medical science cannot explain. The result of "the look" is a paralysis in males. Those in range have been known to stand frozen for hours. Even bystanders have been stunned. In the old West, several bank robberies were reportedly thwarted by strange forces that left the would-be outlaws stuck in their boots. These reports have not been verified by lawmen, but anecdotal evidence supports "the look" directed at the unfortunate outlaws due to said boots tracking mud into the bank. Husbands with pregnant wives should also get used to being startled a lot, as well as being stunned in place by "the look." For practice, they should go quail hunting and watch carefully how the quail are startled when flushed. The husband should then imagine that he is a quail and that his wife is a very angry hunter with a very big shotgun. That should prepare him well for both pregnancy and college tuition.

In scientific (editor's note: he is just guessing) research on TMS, pregnancy was found to cause hormonal overload and emotional outbursts. Why this occurs in males is unknown. I had my first while cooking Hamburger Helper for my wife. I was thinking about how nice it was to be cooking just what my wife wanted when I realized how much it meant to do something for someone who you love and I started crying in my skillet. I instantly tried to share this tender moment with my wife, but she did not get my sentimental feelings. Somehow saying "Sugar, I cried in the Hamburger Helper over you" just does not arouse those tender thoughts in a female, but it does sound like a nice title of a good county music song, though. During pregnancy, cravings for strange food are also common, but why men crave these foods during their wives' pregnancies is not known, but TMS is suspected. During my wife's first pregnancy, I craved two things—chicken fried steak and more food. During the first six weeks of pregnancy, she gained one pound and I gained three.

According to all the pregnancy books, forgetfulness is another common symptom of the condition, but as usual, these books focus only on the mothers and somehow miss the impacts to the fathers. Fathers-to-be who can easily recite statistics from the last twenty Super Bowls can suddenly forget their wives' birthdays. Renowned mathematicians who can expound upon the mysteries of the universe cannot recall their children's names. Some men have even driven to the hospitals without taking their in-labor wives. There are several antidotes to this forgetfulness. These are not medicines that can cure it nor can they even affect it, but they do just as well—they keep the male from getting caught. The solutions require careful planning, preparation, and, of course, blatant deceit. For example, for the forgotten birthday trap, the husband should always have a birthday gift bought and wrapped for presentation. That way, when the wife catches the husband forgetting her birthday, he can just whip out the hidden present and pretend he was just teasing her. If she demands further proof by asking just which birthday it is, he should just look her straight in the eye and say, "Sugar, of course, you are twenty-five", the aforementioned perfect age of females. Getting back to … something. Oh, yeah, forgetfulness. Another way to hide forgetfulness is to confuse the wife. For instance, I have thoroughly confounded my wife with the time and location of our wedding and honeymoon. We were married November 5, 1994; our honeymoon was in Hawaii. I have teased Jeannine many times by saying how we were married November 4, 1995. Gradually, this has sunk in to the point where she gets confused and a little afraid to challenge my own forgetfulness. I also claim that the honeymoon was to Florida. So now she gets really confused and must wonder if I actually have two wives. If I did not look at my marriage certificate at least once a week, I might get really confused myself.

Motherhood brings out the most rational, mature instincts in a female. There is the famous nesting instinct that causes her to prepare her home in advance to the baby's arrival. She does this primarily by excessive cleaning, which is a far cry from Dad's standard "If nothing is growing, it is clean enough." This excessive cleaning is about twice a day and ends immediately after the child is born, because the new mother is much too busy caring for the child (the newborn one and not the one she married). During pregnancy, she also becomes a construction foreman, and a real mean one at that. Her crew is pitiful, which means it consists of her husband. He will paint, clean, drywall, etc. under the stare of a pregnant wife's intolerant eyes. In these endeavors, TMS is very painful to both because it is a well-documented fact that the male eye is oblivious to dirt and clutter in the home. In a garage, barn, or workshop, the tiniest speck may be seen, but in the living space of the ones he loves, a male could not see a greasy tractor rig. Well, maybe he might see the rig if he likes trucks, but he would never see the grease. Anyway, his eye condition is in stark contrast to the wife's nesting instinct which gives her eyes like those of an eagle on steroids while equipped with a telescope. The wife will simply not understand that leaving dirty gym clothes on the floor gives a home "character" and a "lived-in" look. He will not understand painting a room in the contrasting colors of blue and brown. Fortunately, few serious fights develop in these situations, because the female now seems bigger than the male and his instinct to fight or flee naturally chooses the latter. This is why many husbands are often golfing or hunting or fishing during the birth of their children because they were simply too scared to redecorate any longer.

TMS also increases the male sex drive during his wife's pregnancy. Whenever I told my wife she was looking more and more beautiful during her pregnancy, I really, really meant it. However, her changing body knew who had done this to her and immediately sent out the male repulsion hormones to her brain. At least all those cold showers cut down on the air-conditioning bill. But I was lucky; in many species, the female eats the male after mating. The human female does not do this but can come surprisingly close during delivery, and after nine months or so of abstinence, the husband understands perfectly why those male species allow themselves to be eaten.

The medical community did the general populace a real disservice when it began encouraging husbands to go into the delivery rooms, places of great peril for a TMS-infected husband. His interest in gadgets will inevitably lead him to watch the contractions monitor. He will forget to coach his wife's breathing and say such things as "Whoa, here comes a big one!" as if his wife cannot already feel it. He may use his new found expertise in medical equipment to declare "Honey, that one could not have hurt much," despite her screaming that it certainly did and would he like a sample. With that new expertise, he may also expand his practice by remarking about how much worse the contractions will get. Such a comment can make the husband's child an orphan in a hurry, for with the wife's adrenaline pumping, she may grab him and put him in a grip that a professional wrestler would fear. A husband often comes out of a delivery room shaken and very pale, and this is not due to squeamishness but by having his circulation cut off by a very angry and strong wife. Another thing not to say at a time like this is "Just think, dear, you will be going through these two or four more times." The male gynecologist is also not immune to TMS-induced mouth attacks, despite the limited time he actually spends in the delivery room. The delivery room heroines are the nurses who reassure their patients while carefully monitoring the condition (dad's) and, of course, the mother who delivers the baby. The doctors just dash in at the last moment, catch the baby, and then hand the child over to the parents. The doctor may be in the room for all of five minutes. To then say, "Delivering these big babies really wears me out" is not a good idea unless it is simply done to distract the wife long enough to extract her fading husband from her grip. A certain gynecologist once told a certain couple that a nine-pound, five-ounce leviathan with a fourteen-centimeter head was large but not huge. After passing the equivalent of an NFL football out through her body, the wife wanted to know what his definition of huge was. She also wanted some other things, but a husband can be excused from testifying against his wife in a murder conspiracy case, so revealing those incriminating statements is a moot but scary point. There are actually a few good things to say in the delivery room. One is "Honey, I want a vasectomy." She will probably volunteer to perform the surgery herself. With a rusty spoon. However, the best thing to say while in the delivery room is "Honey, he/she is beautiful" when the baby enters this world with a hearty cry. A child is a blessing from God, and a birth is beyond words. Praise God, for these little, big miracles.

Perhaps the most stupid thing to come out of my mouth during my wife's pregnancy was spoken to my sister, the veteran of four kids. I confidently stated that having a baby would not change my life much. After a few minutes of hysterical laughter, my sister rather smugly remarked that, "Oh yes, it will." I am not sure what else I said after that because I was soon digesting them all. Eating those words was not that bad, but eating them in front of my sister was tough. That brings me to an interesting phenomenon. Females can call themselves some pretty coarse things, even accept male agreement, and be perfectly happy, but if a male spontaneously compliments them, they act insulted and get really suspicious. My sister often refers to herself as a good brood mare (a female horse that has had lots of colts for the non-farm types) and readily wants acceptance of that fact. Now, the mother of four kids gets no argument from her brother (who she can still beat up) that raising that big a brood is an impressive accomplishment, but to call my sister a horse and have her like it seems to be courting suicide by sister. Plus, it really does not reflect my true opinion of her. In some weaker and single moments, I told my sister I was looking for a wife with characteristics like her. I told her that I was looking for a beautiful, smart, hard-working woman who would make a wonderful mother. That extreme compliment, coming from a male, and a brother at that, totally blew her mind, because she did not talk to me for a week and requested I lose my membership in the League of Little Brothers Who Torment Their Big Sisters. Still, it revealed a weakness in structure of TMS. The plain truth, when blurted out without thinking, is often the best thing a TMS-affected male can say.

There is an often-quoted statement, "If men had the babies, there would be no more children in this world." A TMS-inspired male offered this rebuttal, "If men had the babies, they would have figured out a better way a long time ago." The male involved will remain anonymous for safety sake unless this researcher is threatened, which would result in him betraying his fellow male researcher immediately. There is the slightest sliver of truth to this dangerous theory that does not involve men having babies or finding a way to do it better. Males are experts at figuring out better ways to do things, primarily if it means getting them out of work or transferring it to others, especially females. This explains why males love technology that does their work for them, and it lets them play with bigger and better toys. What is odd is that males actually helped invent machines that performed what was typically work done by females. Those chores include, of course, virtually all work done on earth and in space, but especially those crudely referred to as housework. The only plausible theory is that these inventions were created as preemptive strikes to ease the day when males would actually be expected to help around the house instead of defending the homestead against marauding marauders, space aliens, and other menaces which also includes actual labor. These machines also freed up the females for more work that was typically done (ignored) by males. The truly remarkable mystery of science is that females both have babies and allow the husbands to live.

In order to ensure his survival, the husband must absolutely not describe the developing child as anything other than "our wonderful baby," and even that is hazardous at times. During our first pregnancy, we first called our child "Peanut" because that was about its size during the first ultrasound. Later, I foolishly and unilaterally suggested the name "Weiner" as its size approached four inches. This did not go over well at all, though I was able to find an acceptable alternative, and "Hot Dog" was it. In our second pregnancy, at about five months, my wife read that the baby was about one foot in length and weighed about one pound. She then described the baby as being the size of a fish. Now, who knows what damage to my person she would have done if I had described our child as a bass. This proved to me very well that Mom may name the child in the womb whatever she wants and not offend anyone, but Dad cannot. Coming up with the formal name is, happily, an acceptable joint venture, and it appears it must be a joint venture because one of the parents inevitably goes insane in the naming game. My wonderfully sensible mother went slightly wacko this way while searching for a name for my sister. To honor my father, whose name is Don, and a furniture line she liked, she suggested Donalee Roweana Henderson. In an action my sister has long appreciated, this name was vetoed, so Kimberly Annette was born. This process has also revealed why females are destined at birth to have better language skills than males. Since typical boy names are short, like Mike, Joe, and Steve, and typical girl names are long, such as Elizabeth, Jessica, and Veronica, girls become very familiar with the alphabet at a very early age, thus developing their communication skills at a very early age.

As a sad aside, our little "Peanut" never lived to reach the "Hot Dog" stage, as we lost this child at about the eighth week. To this day, we maintain a small garden with predominantly white flowers in memory of "Peanut." It had taken us a couple of years to conceive "Peanut," and we were not a young couple at the time. We were confronted with the possibility that children were not to be for us. In God's own miraculous way, He soon answered otherwise. Within six weeks of our miscarriage, we were pregnant with our son Cole. Two more children followed him, and our family was pretty full. I do not understand it all yet, but I do appreciate the true miracle of having a child. The good Lord is in charge, and that is enough.

TMS and Child-Rearing

The male's more mature instincts, if they exist at all, decrease after the birth of their children and tend to direct him into a second childhood. Notice what a proud papa will buy his newborn son. He will purchase "for his boy" such things as a football, basketball, golf clubs, a fishing boat, and an arsenal of hunting rifles, with a lifetime hunting license to boot. The same father who cannot find the world's most famous diapers in the local convenience store will also be able to find and buy the hottest one-inch fishing lure out of the biggest store in America, and on sale no less. The decrease in maturity will also show up in childish rivalry. TMS causes fathers to be very jealous toward their newborns when it comes to mothers' attentions. Daddy will pout mightily if Momma pays no mind to him while she plays with junior or juniorette. He will not understand why his wife is too tired for romance after spending the entire day and night, feeding, dressing, changing, and caring for her "little man." After several days and nights of this "I am too tired tonight, dear," Hubby might even get the message and change exactly one diaper and afterwards expect one really hot night of romance. He will be disappointed, which is another symptom of TMS.

    The husband of a newborn is also very vulnerable to the most basic of TMS impulses. After several months of attempted romance with a pregnant wife, there is something very calming about once again being the larger of the marriage unit. After these many months of abstinence or perceived abstinence, the male will have extremely elevated levels of testosterone—the hormone some believe causes TMS. There is something also very alluring about a wife after seeing her deliver a son or daughter or both. I do not know exactly what it is about sweat, stitches, and clenched teeth that did it, but Jeannine never looked better than after delivery of a large lump of kid. (I guess this explains males' fascination with footballs, which are about the same size.) Unfortunately, a female after delivery of a nine-pound, five-ounce boy is just not very cooperative for some reason, though they remain very powerful and can push through walls and linebacker husbands if separated from their newborn. This strange spirit of aloofness, surely not related to pain or anything that drastic, lasts for a while—like maybe ten years. The TMS-aroused husband is therefore forced by his wife to find solace in another, usually pictures of extended cab pickups.

In extreme cases of marital deprivation, the TMS-plagued husband may get desperate and try to be romantic, whatever that is. No male has ever found out what it is to be romantic with a woman. Cary Grant was reportedly close, but he was an actor and was probably just following a script written by a woman. I have been married for over two decades and I am clueless. My wife has confused me by saying that I am sentimental but not romantic. To me, being sentimental is being romantic, but I guess the desire to collect rocks from places we have visited is somehow not romantic in the female mind. Who does not like rocks? They are solid, look good, and can be used to build stuff, basically what a male thinks he sees in a mirror. The few things wives universally think of as romantic make no sense. An anniversary date in a motel is apparently romantic, but to the TMS-inflicted mind, this is a waste of money for the chance to sleep in a sagging bed in a room that reeks of cleaning supplies. Males generally associate romance with better smells, such as those of new baseball leather or trucks. Females also think sending flowers is very romantic. Why sending dead plants to a female is nice is beyond male comprehension. Flowers may look and smell good, but they fade and drop their petals, an event too similar to what happens to a male's hair and which terrifies his ego. To evaluate the effects of flowers on females, I did bring my wife a rose on our first date, but this was not for romantic purposes, just pure science. The fact that an engineer such as myself was self-aware enough to know most females are not interested in applied calculus also factored in. I figured I was such a boring date that a bribe would be a good way to make a favorable and false first impression. Science and logic won out because only eight years later we were married. I also sent her roses the day of our wedding. Why, I cannot remember, but then again, I, like all males before me, can remember little about the events between the great "will you" and the very permanent "I do." But Jeannine has kept one rose petal from that batch. I do not know if that is her way of being sentimental or romantic, but if it makes her amorous, I do not need to know.

The female has an easier time being romantic. A home-cooked meal with lots of fat is romantic to a male. Saying "Frying chicken sure does make the house smell good" will bring a guy to tears, especially a hungry Southerner. Cheering for the boyfriend's/husband's favorite team is an exceptionally sexy come-on. The college football games demonstrate this perfectly. These games themselves are passionate displays of youthful exuberance filled with school and state pride. Males' emotions rise as they watch in the safety of their living rooms as other males smash each other, effectively eliminating themselves as potential rivals. Half of these rivals fail every play, much to the glee of half the mostly male audience. Commentators dissect their every mistake, further minimizing their football manhood and conveniently ignoring that these highly skilled and conditioned players could squash all the males watching in a second. In addition to all this stimulus, young female cheerleaders dancing around in revealing costumes further fuel futile fits of TMS foolishness, leading to frequent falls and misuse of alliteration. With minds thoroughly muddled and emotionally vulnerable during these moments, males have even resorted to clearly communicating with their significant females, a situation these women play to their advantage to have a meaningful conversation. After a touchdown, a romantic-minded female should throw herself in her guy's arms and tearfully say, "Oh, what a great play! I love you." The guy will reward her emotionally, by looking deeply into her eyes, as long as the replay is not on, and say "Yes it was, and I love you, too." Usually such a public display of emotion is scorned by other males, but when it happens after a big play, or even better after a score, it is acceptable in all male company, even celebrated, as long as a penalty does not erase the good play. Even such a calamity can be overcome by the clever and football-savvy female if she can reflect his instant disappointment back in the form of anger or sorrow. The anger angle is directed at the anonymous referees, whose judgments have hurt the team and, vicariously, the male. By attacking them and defending the team, the female is defending her guy, inspiring both faith and fear, depending on her vocabulary. Expressing sorrow at the pathos of the whole situation indicates tender understanding of the male and the rules of the game, proving her to be of impressive intellect and capable of soothing all his little boo-boos. In addition, the emotional outburst can be cumulative, resulting in every other male in the room looking for his girlfriend or wife. But a word of caution for female readers—make sure his team is the one scoring and make sure to react properly when there are flags on the play to disqualify touchdowns. Acute romantic overtures on a called back touchdown are grounds for divorce in Texas. Romance is simpler in such states as Alabama. Teams from there are usually so good that romantic mistakes are rare and the team usually wins anyway, and that negates past sins. Alabama also usually participates in the championships games played around New Years. This explains why ninety percent of babies born in Alabama are born in Septembers following big bowl game victories. Because I graduated from Oklahoma State University, which is like the Chicago Cubs of college football and went about forty years of losing games to Nebraska and other such teams, romance in football season was more difficult for my wife. Fortunately, other sports will do just as well. Our son Cole was conceived after a particularly good day of water skiing: a sport that is most romantic or sentimental, whichever works.

TMS and Common Characteristics of Good Fathers

Fatherhood is perhaps the most important job and ministry a male will ever have. It is difficult, fun, infuriating, long-lasting, beloved, sorrowful, frightening, and joyful. In other words, it is life at the speed of children, which is faster than the Millennium Falcon at warp factor nine, a description sure to confuse *Star Wars* and *Star Trek* nerds, a state of mind similar to fatherhood at all times. As one with many years of fatherhood, I still do not know much about it, but what I do know is it is a great blessing and my wife is my greatest human ally. In years of research and observation, I have come up with a few indicators of the characteristics of a good father. You know you are a good father if:

- You see an ad for a new vehicle which features a beautiful supermodel—and you notice only the vehicle—and it is a mini-van.
- You scoff when you overhear college students complaining about pulling an all-nighter for an exam. You know what an all-nighter is. A true all-nighter is spent dealing with a two-year-old, a one-year-old, and a pregnant wife all suffering from food poisoning.
- You know exactly how many bedsheets your family has—this due to the aforementioned all-nighter—and the answer is five too few.
- You pass by the local tool department and go straight to the linens—for five more bedsheets.

- You have an accident while rubber-necking a new vehicle—and it is a mini-van.
- You enthusiastically participate in the family Olympics of burping. You are so proud when your one-year-old daughter wins it, because you taught her.
- You discover that the one seat on a John Deere tractor can actually seat three. Notice nothing is mentioned about comfortably seating three. You drive especially carefully because reverse really hurts.
- You know what a BM is. Give yourself extra credit if you know what to do about it.
- You really hate white dress shirts.
- You discover that brown and yellow are your fashion colors—the exact shades of baby food meat and carrots.
- You wear brown-and-yellow paisley ties with brown-and-yellow-striped shirts, because of the above – and nobody minds or gets close.
- Your bass boat is now used to store your kids' toys.
- You buy the car of your dreams—and it is a mini-van. And your wife gets it.
- Your workshop is also used to store your kids' toys.
- Your home office has a crib. It has balloon and sailboat wallpaper.
- You think baby lotion is the most wonderful smell in the world.
- You take your wife out alone on a date and you stop at least twice because the car—a mini-van—seems to sound strange. Then you realize it is just the quiet.
- You take your wife out to a fancy restaurant and still ask what toy comes with the meal.
- You take your wife out on a date and go to the first restaurant that does not come with a playground.
- Your date with your wife includes a movie. For the first time in years, you see a movie without animation.
- You indulge yourself with a little "adult entertainment"—and it is attending your own Sunday school class.
- You regularly play catch with your four-year-old son and know to watch for his low fastball.
- You openly play with your children's toys. Your wife chastises you for not sharing.

- Your two-car garage can fit one vehicle because of your kids' toys. Your dream car—your wife's new mini-van—sits there. Your car—the nine-year-old mini-van—sits in the driveway.
- You know all the nursery rhymes at school and none of the top songs on the radio.
- You really dislike Disney films because they feature smart-aleck kids and dumb dads, which makes the shows seem like reality films.
- You have a cholesterol count that if counted as your IQ, would make you a genius.
- Your golf handicap and waist size are the same—and both are growing.
- You watch your kids' favorite cartoons when they are not around.
- You regularly talk about your infant's "poop."
- You have several years' worth of your kids' photos in your wallet because you cannot stand to remove any of them.
- You decorate your house and office with your kids' artwork. Everyone agrees that they are better than most modern artists.
- You write grocery lists with a crayon.
- You let your kids write on you with their magic markers. You discover later that they are not water washable.
- You like to eat on paper plates.
- You buy children's medicine in bulk and nothing ever expires.
- You lie down with your kids at bedtime to settle them down. An hour later, they are still awake because of your snoring.
- Your kids' car seats have more armor than a tank.
- You think "mortgage" is a dirty word.
- Your teenage daughter comes out of her bedroom dressed like a punk rocker and leaves the house looking like Mother Theresa.
- Your idea of investing in pharmaceuticals is buying children's Tylenol and Benadryl in bulk.
- You are too tired to have a mid-life crisis.
- You look forward to naps.
- You wonder why you hated naps as a child.
- You do all your hunting at the grocery store.
- Your toolbox has as many kid tools as real tools.
- You think Bugs Bunny is still funny.

- You meet all your friends at Little League games.
- You buy your favorite sports team drinks after a game—Kool-Aid drinks.
- You meet your friends again at your pediatrician's office.
- You are really interested in more life insurance.
- You have driven a nail with a kid's hammer because you could not find your own.
- Most of your vehicles run on batteries.
- You know you could design better toys.
- You are learning other languages based on all the assembly instructions found in your kids' toys.
- Going on vacation seems like moving a house.
- You work less at work than at home.
- If a male can see himself in these questions, he is definitely on the right path to being a good father and a patient at a mental hospital.

TMS and Shopping

Females have always been stereotyped as spending machines, but they really are just shopaholics. They can spend so much time in malls that the salespeople know them by name, size, and brand preference, and online they seem eerily connected to the computers, but unlike those scary science-fiction films where artificial intelligence takes over the world, they totally control the computers. This is because while males tend to dominant the electronic world, females naturally dominate males. In addition, women can shop for days without spending any money, sort of like how camels can go for days without water. They tend to shop carefully, too. They hate buying something and then seeing it somewhere else for less. If this happens, they may even return the item at one store and then buy it at the cheaper price at the other. This indicates superior intelligence of an alien origin, or last least alien to males. Perhaps, females really are from Venus, while men originated from primordial ooze and are still trying to become a higher life form.

Males do not shop at malls—they blitzkrieg through them. They know what they want and buy it immediately. Males do not shop around for hours in order to save $5.25. They measure their success in speed. True athletes can get in and out of a mall in under four minutes. And even buy something. Wearable. Does it fit? It depends on location, because a male shopper only notices if something is comfortable in the crotch. Color schemes and how it fits elsewhere can sometimes get neglected. Of course, a male only shops for clothes for himself. With TMS, a male becomes allergic to racks of women's clothes. He also never remembers his girlfriend's or wife's size, and even if he did, he cannot win when choosing a size. If the size is too big, the said female wife will accuse him of calling her fat. If the size is too small, she will say he is calling her too fat by insinuating that this petite size is what she should be wearing. Either way, he will get a lecture on male insensitivity and how all women's clothes designers are sadistic males. This usually trains the male into avoiding buying women's clothes forever. It can also be intimidating just going into a women's department, because most female species are notoriously aggressive when defending their territory, and the women's department is definitely their territory. A NFL linebacker would shrink in fear from a one-half-off rack defended by one petite but snarling female. I once came between a female cousin and a clothes rack. For a while there I was not sure I would make it. Fortunately, I did not come directly in line with something she wanted and I lived to document the dangers of shopping with females.

Males always accuse females of spending more money in the household, and this is often true because a TMS-stricken male counts such minor items as a house mortgage, braces for the kids, food, insurance, doctor's bills, etc. as frivolous female items. He also tends to count each purchase as equal. This makes buying four sixty-dollar outfits equal to buying a fifteen-thousand-dollar fishing boat, a three-hundred-dollar rod and reel, a five-hundred-dollar rifle, and a six-hundred-dollar table saw which he uses once a decade.

TMS also affects a male's eyes while shopping. For instance, a male cannot find baby supplies at all. I personally have never successfully bought baby supplies to date despite being sent many times, and this is due to my eyes not being able to adjust to the light—any light. Once, just after the birth of my son Matthew, my wife sent me out to fill a pain prescription for her. Why she would be needing pain relief after pushing an eight pound plus baby out of her body is a mystery to me, but she did entrust me with this job. I did find the pharmacy. I even managed to hand the female pharmacist the prescription, but I began to unravel when she asked for identification. I had my wallet, but I could not find my driver's license in it. I panicked like a new father should when about to come home empty to a wife in pain. I began to theorize that the reason females of many species eat the males after mating was that the males forgot to bring home pain medication. After stalling and sweating and making two separate and totally unnecessary purchases at the same pharmacy, I finally found my driver's license—in my wallet in the very front in the very same place as I always left it. Needless to say, the lady pharmacist enjoyed filling that prescription, and she probably slipped me some tranquilizers as well.

In addition to medications, certain other baby supplies are nearly impossible for the male eyes to see. Diapers are a prime example. I have been sent to the local Walmart many times for diapers. We used a major national brand in the usual sizes. Somehow, they always seemed to be out of the right size but had all the other sizes in abundance. Fortunately, I was persistent and agile, and with the help of a female associate, I could usually dig up one package in about twenty minutes, but to this day, I have yet to find more than one package of the right kind in the right size in one trip.

Certain things are easy to find by the TMS-infected male. The wrong part for a car is easy to find as well as that bolt that is just one size too large to fix the male's latest project. The right tool for the right job, which is a hopelessly fanciful cliche passed down through countless generations of TMS-affected males, simply does not exist. It is some TMS researchers' opinions, certainly not sane ones, that female engineers and female parts supply managers, all 0.01 percent of the total population, have diabolically specified and supplied conflicting-sized parts and tools for most automobiles, tractors, old trucks, appliances, etc., but this is implausible. For one thing, as any lonely male engineering student will tell you, there are not enough female engineers to accomplish this mission, and the ones that do exist are too smart and too determined to mess with the minds of males, an endeavor well beneath them. Second, females are generally much cleaner than men, a proposition that explains males' fascination with rugby versus ballet, and they would not put up with the clutter of millions of unwanted, well, not wanted, just unusable spare parts lying around. Other researchers have laid the blame on male customer representatives, formerly called salesmen, who developed the theory that males actually like wasting time in hardware stores searching for just the right part and by providing parts of nearly the right size, they can increase overall sales. Unfortunately, this has some merit. Males love standing around other males talking about inanimate objects of steel and iron, a characteristic that explains why mankind (malekind?) has always built idols to worship. This practice made it a good and even holy sacrament to waste time and money with other males doing nothing except avoiding work. Throw in a virgin sacrifice and some liquid spirits, and these early males had invented the perfect Saturday night dream of every fraternity. Other evidence suggests another theory. When males are working on a "project," which they translate as a mission of vast importance to the security of the family unit and, in reality, is just fixing a clogged sink, their patience is usually south of zero. They work hurriedly, anxiously, at night, after-hours, and badly. This is no time for reading directions or even goofing off talking to other males at the hardware store if it is even open. They are like deranged madmen with the flu. Their wives sense their frustration and usually refrain from any criticism of the logic of starting the project without the proper directions, instructions, parts, and tools while herding the kids to her mother's for safekeeping. Meanwhile, the project, which may have involved breaking out an outer wall, is going as well as the husband's temper control, which is as stormy as the approaching West Texas supercell. In this scenario, the trip to the hardware store is a desperate, harrying affair involving the expenditure of lots of money, just like the experience of a family vacation to Disney World. The final and most plausible rationale for problems with these projects suggests that parts and designs are incompatible to their design purposes because males make both. To match parts and designs would take clear and constant communication between a multitude of parties. Since males hate parties without liquor, the design is made without input from potential customers or other sober stakeholders. Part suppliers do not read plans so the proper parts are not stocked. The designers and parts manufacturers are probably not from the same country, so the American design is cleverly done in the metric system, and the German part is done in the English system, and the two principals do not talk to each other because that would be too similar to asking for directions when lost, thus verifying the theory that males cannot find parts at hardware stores because males designed and manufactured their own dysfunction.

Males cannot find females' clothes as well. For instance, some newly married males might try to actually buy their wives gifts from time to time instead of just purchasing gift cards. They eagerly set out to buy their wife a pretty shirt but soon discover there is no such thing. Females wear things called blouses, and they button on the wrong side and have scratchy and uncomfortable fabric. Since male shirts are generally larger, it seems logical that they would cost more than the blouse things, but they cost more. This cost disparity puts the male in a real tizzy and the wife in a tizzy if he happens to buy anything not fifty percent off the sales price. Why is it that only females can find fifty percent off clothes? It must be a conspiracy or eye malady, certainly not male impatience. The shirts or blouses also come in strange varieties of sizes, not just small, medium, and large. For instance, the one-size-fits-all size is usually called petite. Dresses are equally confusing and more expensive. Female pants are called slacks and often do not have a zipper where a male expects it. Logically, a married male should acquire a knowledge of females' clothing, but somehow, he seems to get distracted and never really picks it up. If a male does finally find something he thinks is appropriate, the newly married wife should learn to act happy at the receiving of a nice, soft, very large flannel male shirt. Since the male will leave the tag on and will never notice whether or not the female wears it, returning the gift is easy. Females should just refrain from laughing at these males, at least in their presence, to spare their feelings.

As discussed before, lingerie is a particularly problematic purchase. Younger males are too embarrassed to go near a brick-and-mortar proprietor, and older males are too confused to know what is sold there. Nothing makes sense; lace and straps just do not compute. On their wives, they may look great, but on a shelf, they are just fancy grease rags. As a reminder, females should occasionally check what their husbands use to check the oil in the cars, an event known as an environmental disaster. A slightly useless, very scanty Victoria's Secret's unmentionable will make a good grease rag, especially in front of a crowd of would-be male mechanics. A son might even come in waving it in front of the church ladies social as a proud reminder of his first oil change lesson from his father. For the sake of all humanity, males should never shop for lingerie and just rely upon the typical good judgment of females in dressing themselves and their males they married.

It would seem likely that males could successfully shop via the internet. With high-technology support, surely a simple task as picking out a part or an article of clothing could be accomplished. This is not the case. If an internet site is designed by a female, it would follow female logic, which is sensible and easy to understand. To a male, it is incomprehensible. Since female clothing names are not the same as males', the language barrier is insurmountable for these items. For mechanical parts, males will simply order parts they "know" are correct instead of what some stupid computer tells them is correct. If a site is designed by a male, the language barrier is again insurmountable. A computer male speaks geek, and a mechanical type speaks dork. Both have superiority complexes because the geek makes more money and the dork can crush the geek while neither can talk female. This makes a site designed by a male for female clothes the worst of all. No human has ever successfully navigated a sale from this site; however, a poodle once did.

TMS and Unnatural Attractions

Boat Fever

Typical Male Syndrome may seem rather trivial, but it can be an extremely expensive illness to treat. One of the most expensive symptoms may begin with such an innocent event as a leisurely fishing trip to a local lake. The male may feel the cool breeze as the rental boat glides across the still water. He sees the beauty of a bass exploding upon his lure, and as he reels the fish in from the safety of the fishing chair, he thinks, "Why don't I do this more often?"— and he is hooked, struck down by one of the most powerful symptoms of TMS—boat fever. Boat fever afflicts only males, and while it actually causes no pain to them, it dishes plenty to their wives, as well to the family's pocketbook. The symptoms of boat fever are very severe, causing extreme deterioration in the driving habits of males, because it makes them rubberneck every boat on or near the road and every body of water. They will follow a really good-looking boat for miles, regardless of their actual destination. Not all the symptoms are negative, because boat fever does improve reading skills dramatically due to all of the time males spend reading want ads, internet listings, and boat catalogs. The local marina operator will become their best friend and closest confidante. As in other documented TMS cases, eyesight becomes very limited. For example, unafflicted males looking at boat ads would see the beautiful female models and perhaps even the price tags. A male with boat fever would only see a Cajun 1800 fish and ski, 150 hp Johnson outboard, 18' long, beam 90, etc.

This author must confess to having had this condition. Early in my marriage, I wanted a boat baaaddddd. I tried to justify it to my wonderful wife Jeannine by saying it was for her, but she was not convinced. I calculated the economics of the purchase and found it was really a wise investment, and she, an accountant by trade, claimed it did not compute. I tried to explain that by assuming two dollars a pound for fish, all I had to do was catch enough fish to eat three times a day for 71.7 years to pay for the boat. Jeannine, the ultraconservative CPA, just did not believe my numbers. I finally convinced her with my logical and rational arguments, accompanied by incessant whining.

After looking for about a month, I saw a boat that we both liked. We decided to make an offer. I, being a cool, calculating customer would do the dealing. The salesman began to talk about the 1993 blue-green 1750 Cajun Espirit with the 115 hp Yamaha outboard while I drooled on the boat. He talked about the live wells; I began calling the boat soft, feminine names. The salesman realized the situation and began talking religion. He asked me if I would take good care of her and I said I would. He asked for any objections, but there were none. Gravely, he pronounced us man and boat, and then he broke down and cried while passing an old plate to take my money. I kissed the boat as a tear slipped down my feverish cheek. Jeannine, my usually understanding wife, seemed jealous, and said, "I married a five-year-old nut."

I was now the proud owner of a used boat. There is an old saying that the two happiest days of a boat owner's life is the day he buys it and the day he sells it. I can testify that the former is true, because I spent that first day on cloud nine and cannot remember much of it. Now, an interesting thing about boat fever is that it makes males even more oblivious to facts and reality in general. I did not mention how I pulled the boat home or where I stored it because I owned no vehicle capable of pulling a boat and I did not have any room to store it—minor details for sure when buying a boat. Luckily, my father-in-law supplied both a pick-up and a storage shed that I had recently helped him build. Looking back, I am simply amazed that he asked me to do this about the same time I started talking about getting a boat, though I did notice he and Jeannine exchanging what seemed to be smirks while I pounded nails in for the roof in ninety-five-degree heat and humidity.

About three weeks after the 1750 Cajun fish and ski treatment, the boat fever began to subside, especially when shown our bank statement. Although successful, the treatment illustrated the pain of boat fever because of its cost.

The fever has also tended to subside each time something went wrong with the boat or when I spent more than two hours fishing in one-hundred-degree heat without a bite or sunscreen. My recommendation for avoiding boat fever is simple: keep males away from water deeper than bathwater and never ever let them fish.

Motor Vehicles

TMS causes males to have many other unnatural attractions besides to boats. This is not believed to involve sexual connotations; however, the way some males look with lust at a MOTOR VEHICLE makes this a difficult call. Make, model, or age of the vehicle does not matter. Males can swoon over an old clunker just as easily as over a new Corvette, but pickups cause the worse outbreaks. A new pickup shown to a boys' gym class will cause more collisions and arguments than a supermodel swimsuit magazine. The preference for certain kinds of pickups generates more controversy than religion for males, because one can be either a Ford truck man or a Chevy truck man, never both. A Chevy truck-driving Catholic would rather be baptized by immersion a million times than drive a Ford. A Ford truck-driving Baptist would say a thousand Hail Marys before he would set foot in a Chevy, while Dodge truck owners are pitied by the other two brand drivers as just too poor to own a real truck. A Ford or Chevy man also does not understand the religion of a foreign truck owner at all and considers them as part of a really pathetic cult. Females are invisible riders in trucks, and even a supermodel can get thrown out of a truck show if she obstructs the view of the extended cab. There is also anecdotal evidence of female invisibility which involves an extremely jealous husband of a beautiful woman. They were parked at a gas station in his extended cab 4x4 when the husband heard this long whistle. He stormed out and confronted another male who was obviously in love. He was about to fight the other man when the guy asked if his truck had a 350 V8, and they have been best friends ever since. Some male historians have theorized that if Helen of Troy had been just been traded for a pickup truck, there would not have been a Greek-Trojan war, unless, of course, the token truck was a Honda.

As males age (they do not mature, for they are born as mature as they get), their TMS problems with automobiles worsen. Even an old curmudgeon gets that look in his eyes when he spots a vehicle he likes. Some males near death have recovered and lived for years after inspecting the hearse that was to carry them to the cemetery. Middle age seems to be an especially vulnerable time because some males at this time of their lives revert to early adulthood stages and become fascinated with sports cars. They may even start acting like the Casanovas they never were. Being beset with TMS, they cannot see that any color of a convertible Corvette contrasts horribly with their gray hair and toupee of many colors. The sharp lines of a Trans Am also do not go well with the rounded lines of a middle-aged belly. Fortunately, they age out of this quickly enough, and by the grandfather stage, they get over TMS sports car fever when more practical things like nice comfortable seats become the primary consideration, though other factors like actually being able to get out of the seats without help also aid the recovery. These males also readily appreciate a ride that does not rattle their dentures and gravitate toward sales pitches involving "touring sedan," "plush seats," and "roomy interiors." They will actually inspect the trunk of a new car to ensure it has sufficient luggage space for a month-long visit with the grandkids. But there is one vehicle that inspires passion in later years—the riding lawnmower. Grandfathers love riding lawnmowers and consider it a male rite of passage to drive a riding lawnmower in baggy shorts, black socks, and old dress shoes, while often carrying passengers such as grandkids. It is thought that the first riding lawnmower to offer drink holders was designed for these males. Market research suggests that as millennials age, they will demand lawnmowers with air-conditioned cabs and the latest assortment of electronic devices. I say, "Bring it on!"

Fathers do not get as excited about riding lawnmowers because they are more concerned with growing children than growing grass. Besides, if the kids are old enough, they do the mowing and with a push mower, but if they are too small, that duty may be delegated to the wife who at least merits self-propelled push mowers. Occasionally, the husband of very young children and a pregnant wife whose doctor says she cannot mow the lawn is faced with doing the yard by himself, a tragedy that explains the popularity of lawn services. A younger father also has different tastes toward cars as well, with a strong preference for four doors versus four-barrel carburetors. These males will get excited over cars such as vans, station wagons, sports utility vehicles, and other multi-passenger types of automobiles, but not sports cars. Gas economy gets more drools than the statistics of going zero to sixty in a few seconds. Crash tests results are investigated closer than the swimwear issue of *Sports Illustrated*. For the very young, single males, sports cars are the obsession, although they are even more interested in the above-mentioned issue of *Sports Illustrated* but are too poor to afford either. These males must take what they can get, driving used four-door cars sold to them by their mothers while they dream of sports cars that none of them can buy, at least until they are ready for a mid-life crisis.

Another unnatural attraction caused by TMS is associated with male hobbies. One hobby is tool and implement collecting because males, like magnets, seem attracted to metal objects. The most expensive tools and farm equipment cause the most attraction, as witnessed at county fairs where urban city-dwellers swoon over new tractors and monster trucks. The bigger vehicles could swallow their entire houses, yet they still long to buy them. Fortunately for their wives, these bad boy toys cost more than their homes, and a dollar sign with six figures behind it can penetrate even the worst TMS-infested brains. Research has shown that males do not necessarily use these tools and equipment; they just collect them. The cause of this obsession is not fully known, but most researchers theorize that just as pregnant females tend to "nest" and fix up their home in anticipation of the baby, males tend to "nest" by filling their garage and storage sheds with metal objects. The weight of this nest would bend over a redwood, and any chicks raised there would likely get impaled, but the father bird would still exhaust himself looking for just the right angle iron. As a human example of nesting, the family farm where I grew up had many barns and sheds, and all were filled with a multitude of tools, implements, and scrap metal, much of which were for use with draft horses. My grandfathers and father just refused to throw anything away, but I seemed to have escaped this particular affliction at all, and the fact that I have a brand-new router in my shed that I have never used does not prove anything. Some say denial is a symptom of TMS, but I have found no evidence. Editor's note: I have!

This affinity for collection makes certain stores, websites, and mail-order catalogues especially hazardous to the family's pocketbook. My mother must have hated those John Deere catalogues and one reason was my father built a new barn fifteen years before renovating their home, whose porch was literally falling in. I do not have this symptom either, although I did want to get registered for our wedding at Home Depot and my wife strangely thought that was a bad idea. Did I mention that some say denial is a symptom of TMS?

Golfing

A passion for golf is a sure sign of a male suffering from TMS. Another brave but deceased researcher suggested that TMS sufferers seek relief from females by taking up this sport. His thinking was why else would a perfectly sane male spend four to five hours of a weekend and countless dollars trying to beat a pock-covered ball into a hole, before lying about his score, how much fun he had, and about how much beer he drank? The late researcher reasoned, or nearly reasoned, that this isolation from the female species lessened the effects of TMS, but he ignored that females also golf, as evidenced by how often males complain of a group of ladies holding them up on the golf course, especially when these ladies play better than they. Other wiser and still living researchers think natural instincts explain golf. Males have yet to evolve past the hunter/gatherer social mentality. In a complicated, computer-nerd world, golf fulfills this basic need, fore! on a golf course, a male must hunt and hunt and hunt to find his ball (conveniently shaped and colored to resemble a food item—an egg). He takes the tools of the game, again not by accident called clubs, to systematically beat this ball (an egg by emotional transferal) into a hole, which is analogous to a cave, the typical gathering place of prehistoric food stuffs. The hypothesis concludes the fudging on the golf scorecard comes from the cavemale's natural instinct to lie about why they missed the Wooly Mammoth and instead mark it down as a kill in their cave drawings. Most female researchers of TMS agree with this theory, but strangely conflate the similarities of prehistoric cavemales with their modern counterparts.

Most wives view their husbands' golfing in two ways. One is to look at it as four to five hours of glorious freedom from their eldest child, better known as their husband. Another view is that golf is just another male way to get out of work. In most families, males fear the truth in the first viewpoint and vigorously deny the truth in the second. The first theory recognizes females must rest various neutrons of the cortex cerebrum thingy, else cellular biodegradation occurs, which in non-medical terms means they need a break or they go nuts. The second theory rests on the proposition that males are just lazy, but researchers with naturally unbiased opinions (males who surely do not have the TMS symptom of self-delusion) most vehemently deny the view that golf is just goofing off. They first declare this ancient, respected sport is very good exercise, because getting out of those golf carts with their padded seats is very difficult, and considering where most males hit the ball, golf usually consists of rock climbing, trailblazing, and occasionally swimming to boot. Besides these activities, the heart really gets a cardiovascular workout when a ball is sailing over an expensive subdivision. In addition, most males consider golfing dedicated practice for second careers on the Senior Players Golf Association professional tour. This later career is the reason I golf, and I most certainly do have the self-delusion symptom of TMS.

Deer Fever

Another symptom of TMS is deer fever. According to cardiovascular specialists, males get more excited seeing a deer while hunting than they do when having sex. These researchers discovered that males' hearts race when they spot a deer and that many heart attacks occur while hunting. This aroused level of excitement is a very dangerous symptom of TMS, not only for the male but also for the female. In some rare but tragic attempts to get noticed by their husbands, some females have gone into their bedrooms dressed like deer, not comprehending that males consider anything moving in deer season as possible prey and shoot accordingly, following the motto "If it is brown, it is down." Fortunately, most TMS-inflicted husbands simply are not used to getting that excited at home without a football game being shown on TV and their usual reflexes are too slow to cause any damage to anything more dangerous than a turkey leg with dressing. To biased researchers (females), deer fever is an irrational response to TMS, because sitting frozen for hours in a tree waiting for a deer to come by to be shot is not normal, even for a male. First, these researchers reason, most hunters, after sitting for hours in the early morning cold, are too stiff to shoot. Second, if the hunter actually succeeds in bagging a deer, that means hours of work processing the kill, something suspiciously close to cooking and cleaning which usually causes allergic reactions in males. Finally, the researchers observe that after all is done, the male can only point to an amount of meat easily obtained by one trip to the grocery store. The female researchers fail to compute that "natural" meat obviously lasts longer and provides much more nutrition than other types of meat. The fact that venison has a gamy taste that limits the proportions most can choke down has nothing to do with it. Remarkably, as "wild game," the males actually insist on cooking it with their typical ineptitude, further extending the freezer life of his manly provisions while providing the females a handy excuse to call for takeout at their favorite restaurants. One of the rare features of deer fever is it may cross species/gender lines and infect human females, resulting in hunters with incredible shooting skills and even better culinary talents. In the south, married females of this kind are known as "trophy wives."

In stark contrast to male deer hunters, fishermales are immune to TMS. It is true, the feel of a bass striking a lure raises a male's heart rate to over 227 beats a minute, but this is just a natural reaction to potential food being procured for the hungry family, and just because the sight of a line knifing back and forth through the water causes fishermales to droll does not mean they are subject to TMS. This response is just due to the adrenalin of primal man's instincts to fight or flee, and in this case to fight the ferocious six-ounce bass. Plus, as fishermales will testify, nothing beats fried fish to eat (editor's note: unless it is beef, chicken, or pork). The most in-depth science confirms fishermales do not have TMS despite the time spent away from work, the costs of gear and bait, the slightly exaggerated (editor's note: outrageous lying) tales of the catch. I confess I am personally more of a fishermale than a deer hunter, yet I have found no symptoms of TMS involving this sport. (Editor's note: except self-delusion.)

My sons, Cole and Matthew, are deer hunters, but are only slightly infected by TMS, as am I. The mild infection began with our first hunt together. Now, the year before that, they had gotten pocket knives for Christmas and were both bleeding profusely before my wife and I were even up, but despite this experience, I, as a responsible parent, decided to increase the lethality of the presents the next Christmas by buying them a one-shot deer rifle and a bow (without the ammunition and arrows at my wife's insistence). That next fall, they were ready for their first hunt. In Oklahoma, the state wildlife department sponsors a special youth weekend which is a time when only youth can hunt with rifles, while accompanied by a responsible adult, which apparently included me. The youth must pass a hunter's certification test put on by the department which consists of a program that not only emphasizes gun safety at an early age, it also trains young ones on hunter ethics. It is a very thorough training session, covering all likely subjects the student needs, to make safe and responsible decisions, unlike the standard instructions given to new parents which consist of "Here is your baby." With this government-mandated training, the only known government program known to be effective, the new hunter and a legal guardian (angel?) are ready to face the wild outdoors, except when the last name is Henderson. Even with the preparation, no one in our family was really prepared for our first hunt together. We arrived at the deer stand, basically a porta-potty, at 0715 (I use military time to let the reader share the mood of danger). I know the exact time because I thought then I would be back at approximately 1030, enjoying a delicious breakfast of biscuits and gravy, cooked by my mother-in-law for her tired and brave little hunters, with me thrown in just because. But after a few minutes, my younger son Matthew began claiming he saw a deer. Since my son was young and rather imaginative, I discounted his claim. A few more minutes went by and he again insisted he saw one. This went on for a few iterations until I finally was able to squeeze around the crowded porta-potty and actually look out. There was not just one deer; there was a herd of them. It was Cole's turn to shoot and he excitedly asked me, "Can I shoot? Can I shoot?" This was my first hunt too, but I wanted to give him confidence, so I assuredly said, "Sure." He shot and missed. Deer are clever and skittish creatures with great instincts and speed and with the shot, these quickly scattered into the woods, and I figured that was it. In about five minutes, though, the herd reappeared and Cole had reloaded and was ready. He fired, and a deer stumbled; the herd again scattered into the woods. I know we needed to wait before tracking the wounded deer, so we stayed put in the porta-potty stand. It was now Matthew's turn to shoot, though he knew the clever deer would not return after two shots and he would not be getting a shot. Apparently, the deer did not understand any of this and again returned to the open area right in front of our hunting stand. Matthew now shot and missed and the deer ran away for the third time in twenty minutes. After about fifteen minutes, Cole and I left the stand to begin the tracking process, but before we went ten feet, Matthew called out that the deer were back again! I hurried back to the stand and tossed him another bullet. He took careful aim while announcing, "This one has blood on it." He fired and cried out, "I got it!" Again, I figured he was just too excited to be accurate, but I walked over to the edge of the ridge and, to my surprise, I looked down to see a dead deer. On closer examination, I saw it had been shot twice. My boys had shot the same one, which to this day we call the "Suicidal Deer." The time was now 0830, breakfast would have to wait, and deer fever had seized our entire family.

Entertainment and TMS

Typical Male Syndrome affects what is watched on the family television. Most uneducated people think males only watch football games, fishing shows, and the news (only the sports segments), but males also appreciate classical movies, which is basically anything with John Wayne in them. TMS researchers have correlated that the movie *She Wore a Yellow Ribbon* will soon rival *Hamlet* in future artistic circles. They also predict John Wayne movies will someday immortalize American culture the same way all those busted buildings and cracked, half-naked statues make Greece so revered in the arts world. Males also go for educational TV and will watch the Weather Channel for hours, studying the map in search of dangerous storms that could endanger their families or stir up the fishing. Just because they appear dazed and incoherent while staring at the screen does not mean they are not lonely and vigilant sentinels, ever prepared to fight the perils of an approaching cloud. "No," researchers conclude, their gaze is just the typical lonely sentinel look, which is also a warning to not ask them any important questions during their vigil, because during these types of experiences, males may give some slightly strange answers, due, of course, to their extreme concentration to the television. For instance, a male immersed in the Weather Channel might be asked what he thinks of the new preacher and the response "all wet" might not be his actual opinion but is actually next week's forecast, at least that is the hope. During a far north nature special on large carnivores, a wife once asked her husband how she looked in her new dress. Suffice to say, "like a grizzly bear" was not a good response. There is some good news in all of this, though. Meteorologists have been wise to name hurricanes actual human names, which has greatly helped males with those untimely questions about what to name future sons and daughters. Some warning, though, because not all the hurricane names are gender-neutral, and it is not recommended to name a daughter Fred nor boy Sue unless they will be lawyers, an occupation born to antagonize.

TMS also causes males to maximize the television experience by watching several shows at once. Some females scornfully call this "channel surfing," but males call it efficiency. On a really productive evening, a male can watch about seven channels at once. This is especially important during football season, as this allows one to catch virtually every game on TV. Unfortunately, the eyes of females cannot focus during changes in channel, causing headaches and irritability, which is usually directed at the blissfully viewing male. This sensitivity to changing channels is called "Channel Surfing Deficiency Syndrome," and denial of this disease is rampant among its female sufferers.

Males do not understand female romance novels or so called "women movies," but the cause may not be TMS but Freudian logic. "Women movies" are only seen on weird stations on TV, typically including in their names such words as "family," "life," "educational," etc. in them. These shows are only viewed by married people, because single males surf right through them, and single females cleverly keep them off the TV until after marriage, when the remote gets lost and shows such as *I Lost My Husband, but I Understand Myself Better* appear. These movies have plots that would give Freud writer's block because they have no logical flow and never have an ending. The typical plot is something like this—a woman has unfulfilled dreams, generally about some artsy career in which her great aunt (who regularly talks to cats) says she is gifted. The female sacrifices her imaginary career for the man she loves. They have two kids, no more, no less, and always a boy and a girl. The boy fights with the dad and the girl fights with the mom, before everyone instantly reconciles. The mother now has a deeper understanding of herself. And then the husband dies suddenly. The end. Huh?

The romance novel is very similar to the "woman's movie." In fact, they are usually adapted for made-for-TV movies shown only on the "Life Is so

Bittersweet Channel." Males usually find these novels interesting at first glance at the half-naked female on the cover but never dare to pick them up or heaven forbid read one. Their interest also quickly wanes as there is always a half-naked man on the cover as well. It is unknown why these figures are actually on the book covers as such scenes are never described. In addition, the males in the books are always mysterious artists or writers and never TMS-infected engineers or accountants, the types of males, who, statistically speaking, make enough money to raise a family and whose idea of a mid-life crisis is to secretly attend a Comic-Con convention as a *Star Wars* character. The artist and writer types, based on extensive physiological testing (in junior high gym classes), could not bench press a puppy, much less literally sweep a female off her feet. It would take the use of a front-end loader for these types of guys to lift those ladies, and artist types cannot even operate a mechanical pencil, so something that actually has an engine would be way too difficult. To sweep a female off her feet, the mindful accountants would hire some weightlifters to do the job, while logical thinking engineers would build a catapult. It is true, some of the male figures in the novels are part-time tradesmen who could hoist an opera singer and her accompanying piano, but it strains the male readers' imaginations, assuming males had imaginations and would read a "women's novel, to believe a gorgeous female with tons of money would so much as speak with the barely working male in these novels or would actually marry the bum who cannot hold down a full-time job. These theories and concepts are accepted as 100 percent true despite the lack of corroborating evidence. Due to the unlikelihood of a male ever reading a romance novel, such data may never come.

Chick-flick movies are far different from woman movies. Chick flicks can be tolerated by the average male due to the fact that they make for great dates. Going to these movies makes the male look very romantic, and the comedy involved, usually caused by something silly the TMS-infected male star does, is funny for the female who understands it and the male who does not realize he does or will do things just as dumb. In addition, these movies tend to have a somewhat sane plot and always have an ending where the male does not die and the screen couples make out, right before the viewing ones do, much to the male's delight.

The differences in entertainment also extend to talk shows, which TMS-infected males avoid but females enjoy, especially the ones with lots of emotional outbursts. The ratings for these shows seem to be based on volume of tears shed, not counting the ones shed by males who have lost the remote or cannot find the channel changer button on the set. Scorning the psychological torture of these emotional talk shows, males stir toward more educational topics, brilliantly analyzed in-depth on pre-game, halftime, and post-game sports interview shows. These feature lots of male talk about the latest crack-back block or illegal procedure, though there are occasional emotional outbursts, though rooted in situations comprehensible to males. For example, if an athlete wins big in something and gets kissed by a girlfriend, he is allowed to cry, especially if showered in alcoholic beverages which are likely burning his eyes anyway. Obviously, these shows are way different from female talk shows because these are called "interviews" or even some intellectual term like "report." These shows involving males analyzing the mangling of other males reach some higher plane of communication that females just do not ride. A certain sarcastic female researcher named Jeannine even suggested that it was a lower form of communication dating back to the cavemales who cheered as cavemale Bubba weaved and dodged around a wooly mammoth. She theorized the cave drawings were sports page statistics of the local hero's exploits, which also explains why most of the drawings seem to be of such ferocious creatures as deer and lizards. She also supposes that when "wooly" was the victor, the local chisel editors conveniently forgot that day's edition of Stone Age Sports Center. This researcher rejects such theories as he looks forward to the analytics of next week's Hemorrhoid Bowl game.

There are also male-dominated talk shows that involve "the news." These shows are not about emotional outbursts, despite the yelling and red faces. The ratings are also not based on the volume of tears, despite those shed by the few viewers with triple-digit IQs or basic human decency. These shows feature many males who were chosen last in gym class and figured life owed them something after that, in other words, politicians. It would be tempting to assign TMS as a driving force behind these shows and the reactions of the participants, but even TMS symptoms are too rational to explain these things.

A TMS-infected male does have his favorite television shows, and as expected, they involve sports. On Sunday afternoons, a favorite show for males is any golf match. Females have no clue about the joys of watching golf, despite the popularity of the LPGA tour. Just because nothing seems to happen in golf does not mean that it is not enjoyable either. Seeing other males battle Mother Nature in such an historic sport gives males a sense of sacred continuity. This contentment is very emotional, and males, being the tough guys that they are, cleverly disguise their outbursts by pretending to sleep during most of the telecast. Watching golf, with its subtle mental challenges, also inspires strategic thinking, best done with the eyes closed. This is important because a TMS infection is very painful and requires a great deal of strategic thinking to overcome its effects. Strategic thinking should never be confused with napping, which is usually done while the wife is speaking, and normally about when will the male fix the leaky faucet or mow the yard.

In old movies, soldiers were often depicted as macho, single males saving the world from the Nazis while adoring, beautiful, and equally single females fall helplessly in love with them. However, in extensive studies of American war heroes conducted at the prestigious bastion of higher learning (Bixby High School), it is clear that most American war heroes (at least the officers) were old married men. Some TMS researchers, soon to be deceased, have developed the theory that being married makes men more experienced in battle and better equipped to develop strategies that lead to survival. They are certainly trained to retreat, which is especially useful if confronted by an unexpected slumber party of middle school girls. The researchers suggest that instead of military training at expensive public institutions, our national security would be better served if our soldiers simply trained at home. One soon-to-be-maimed researcher has stated, "An army of married men with teenage children would be invincible because they have seen all forms of warfare." This assumes the opposing army does not also consist of married men with teenagers, which if it did would result in a draw with no shots fired because the dads would never disturb the quiet and would spend the precious free time watching golf and thinking strategically. My only opinion on the matter is that if married men really are better soldiers, it is only because they have the best things to serve and protect.

TMS and Acronyms

Significant Male Other (SMO) and Significant Female Other (SFO) are research terms for male and female pairs who interrelate on a frequent and personal basis, and sometimes, they even talk to each other. On very rare occasions, they even listen. SMOs are husbands, boyfriends, sons, and brothers; SFOs are wives, girlfriends, daughters, and sisters. When a SMO and SFO really get together and actually marry, the result is often a pack of Significant Little Others (SLOs).

The acronym SMO may get confused with the acronym for Health Management Organization, or HMO. The terms sound similar so a comparison is in order. HMOs are supposed to save money but cost dearly, as do SMOs. HMOs are for good health, and SMOs cause their SFOs much pain, stress, and other health disorders. HMOs drive people crazy, while SMOs drive only their SFOs crazy. HMOs are regulated by Congress, which is full of TMS-infected SMOs who love acronyms. SMOs are regulated by SFOs who love their SLOs so much that they do not kill their SMOs.

TMS and Pets

TMS affects a male's choice of pets. Real men like dawgs, big dawgs. No self-respecting man would walk a poodle; in fact, no self-respecting man ever walks a dog period, they walk with the dawg. Real dawgs for real men are closely in touch with their primitive past; real dawgs are huntin' dawgs or guarding dawgs. A real dawg is constantly on the prowl, ever ready to attack some…tomato plants. Real dawgs hunt everything and are particularly proficient at hunting and killing shoes. They know their brands, too, always going for a $150 pair of Nike's over a worthless slipper. They see TV cable lines as vicious snakes, and chew accordingly. Garden plants are viewed as mortal enemies, and boat brake cables make for a favorite snack. Real dawgs also love to chase and bark at squirrels, never catching them but surely damaging their prey's hearing with their barking. Dawgs seem to think that squirrels will drop dead out of a tree by just the sound of their barking, but squirrels know the exact jumping capability of their noisy adversary and will provoke real dawgs incessantly by climbing to that limb just out of the dawg's reach. They will then sit and chatter at them. TMS-infected males are very sympathetic to the dawgs because it reminds them of conversations with their significant female others. The dawgs will respond by more, louder barking. Females will see the scene and be sympathetic to the squirrels because this reminds them of conversations with their significant male others . The dogs will then attempt the typical male solution to a problem—

a home improvement project consisting of digging out the tree the squirrels are in. The tree is usually massive and would require a D-10 bulldozer to remove, but dawgs just do not understand construction, just destruction. Again, the females see the similarities in their male loved ones and their dawgs and both species' non-skill at home improvement. With luck and proper female instruction on handling a shovel to fill a hole, the dawg project at least is kept in check.

As briefly mentioned before, females have very different tastes in pets. The typical pet for a female is a house cat, the most illogical creature on earth beside the human fexxxx (editor's note: this word was stricken due to readers' sensibilities and for the author's own darned good). House cats are persnickety, destructive, moody, arrogant creatures that think they own humans. They think they are so independent, yet they have to have their own poop box as if the great outdoors is not good enough. They demand everything and are never around when the human wants to pet them if, for some reason, any rational human would even want to pet a cat. There is one breed of cat acceptable to males—the legendary barn cat. Barn cats are truly independent but without an attitude about it. They are like the early pioneers—tough, rugged, individualistic, and a little smelly. These characters actually work for their living, eating mice and other varmints that infest a real man's barn while never demanding attention nor affection. If "old Barney" catches a mouse, he will not proudly drop it right in front of a human for inspection like a house cat. No, "old Barney" eats the thing. If a real man has a TMS attack in the barn, and searches the whole place for the screwdriver in his back pocket, the barn cat will not be seen gloating. A house cat, though, was born with a sneer on its face and just loves to taunt males over any botched home improvement project. It is no wonder that house cats are often locked accidentally outside on rainy nights.

Horses are another animal that can indicate the level of TMS in an individual. Horses sense the disease and pick their riders accordingly. If the horse likes to ride the range, get lots of fresh air, and generally harass the dumbest animal on earth, the cow, it will inevitably pick a male as its mount. This horse will be tough, rangy, sure-footed, and smart—it has to be smart because its usual rider is not and would chase cattle all over the good green earth in all kinds of weather for no reason at all. In circumstances similar to a hurricane or F-5 tornado, the horse and the ever faithful cow dawg will team up and act skittish and whine a lot, sort of like a normal cat. The male rider will notice these "animal signs," while ignoring the howling winds and frequent lightning strikes, and will decide not to get the cattle up that day because Mother Nature is telling him "a storm's a'brewing" while the Weather Channel blares tornado warnings in the background. His wife, who has been watching the Weather Channel talk about the coming storm for two days, will agree and even rave about her husband's knowledge of the great outdoors. His ego properly stroked, the husband will stride out to the outdoor workshop to do a few "rainy day" chores she has asked him to do for a year. Of course, he will return five minutes later, drenching wet, after having forgotten his raincoat.

If a horse cannot tolerate TMS, the animal and a prospective female rider will mutually understand and quickly bond. This horse will be as pampered, groomed, and as persnickety as a cat. In fact, this horse is basically a large, more expensive cat that can seat a female and unseat a male. For its female companion, this horse is comfortable to ride and will handle nicely in the curves, just like a sensitive sports car. For a male, this horse is hard to start and will pitch uncontrollably upon acceleration. Upon mounting this type of horse, a male will promptly execute an impromptu dismount, flopping at the female's feet, an appropriate place, and will instantly get a lecture about hurting her horse. This lecture may last right up to admittance to the emergency ward.

A TMS-infected male may have the characteristics of many common pets. A bad husband or boyfriend is just like a cat. He looks good, moves smoothly, is totally debonair, devoid of true affection, and is rotten to the core. This male will carouse all night and then come in howling at 3:30 A.M., waking up later at noon and totally ignoring his mate and kittens while somehow making them feel everything is their fault. He is a guileful guilt trip on two legs. In contrast, a good husband or boyfriend is like a dog. He is loyal, dependable, poorly groomed, protective, slightly slovenly, and only bites when someone threatens his owner. Scratch him behind the ears and he is yours for life; feed him well and he will never be late for dinner; and scratch his tummy and he will fall into a contented sleep in two minutes. He rarely has accidents inside the house, not counting home improvement projects, and never barks at night—snoring is another matter. Wink at him and he will wag his tail; praise him and he will do tricks such as take out the garbage or wash the car. He may slobber some, but this is a sign he is happy and content, but be gone from home too long and he may rebel by messing up the house with another home improvement project. He is the happiest when he is with his mate and puppies. May all females have dogs for mates.

In Sickness and in Whining

It is well known that males and females have vastly different pain tolerances. What is not as well known is that males have different situational pain tolerances. For instance, no male has ever gotten sick during the Super Bowl, except when his team is losing; however, emergency room admittances go up dramatically during major network showings of *Gone with the Wind* and other "women movies." Males can also withstand great extremes of temperature in certain situations. Male deer hunters can sit for hours up in trees in subzero temperatures with no ill effects, except they may have to be chipped out of the tree stands. They suffer no maladies except for a propensity for telling even wilder lies about the deer they almost shot. In contrast, these same males will not be able to rake leaves in the yard, because at fifty degrees Fahrenheit with a five-mile-an-hour wind blowing, it is too cold for yard work. These males can, however, smash each other's bones in football or basketball in the same weather conditions, calling it "playing with pain." A male will even remain best friends with the guy who just sent him to the osteopath with a sprained ankle and seven stitches, but when his wife asks him to please help out fixing dinner, he will pout and complain for weeks when he cuts himself while slicing potatoes, and the look he gives his wife when she says "That can't hurt too bad, there isn't any blood!" would shame the poutiest child. He will then mightily squeeze his little finger until he produces a speck of blood to justify further pouting while protesting "It is too bleeding!" He will then thunder to the medicine cabinet and loudly dispense with doctoring himself with iodine and multiple layers of bandages. After Dr. Husband returns, he lectures his wife, who has passed the equivalent of three footballs, his children, out of her body with no pain medicine, on the severe pain he has endured with his scratch.

Males and females also react differently when they are sick. Females want to be left alone when sick which affords them one of the few times they can catch up on their sleep. This conflicts with the husband's mismatched "mothering instinct." The husband thinks a little tender loving care will help her recover quicker and get back to mothering the kids and him. His hovering over her bed results in less sleep and more irritation to the entire household, but it does have therapeutic value in that the wife recovers faster in order to avoid her pestering husband. The TMS-afflicted husband, like most males, gets very sick when germs come calling. Some researchers theorize males really have about the same tolerance for pain as females but are generally bigger, so therefore they get more and bigger germs. When a male gets sick, he reverts back to his natural and historic instincts having been bred and conditioned to look to Mommy when hurt, so he will naturally want to be babied when sick. These natural instincts are not recognized by wives at all. Their reactions to their full-grown husbands' cries for mercy are met with sarcasm and very little compassion. These same females, who rush their infant sons to the hospital if they miss one feeding or get one sniffle, show no feelings to their husbands' sufferings with "bronchial infections with complications" (i.e., a cold, but a pretty baaad one).

Typical Male Syndrome also makes males painfully sensitive to certain types of bad language, but that does not mean they faint at the sound of a cuss word. Substandard use of the English language does not cause any pain either, and in fact, quality of grammar is considered inversely proportional to true manhood. The type of language that really reduces a male to the status of a shaking addict is the strange tongue uttered at baby showers. There is no place on earth that can match the unhealthy sugar content of a baby shower chorus of females admiring gifts. Each gift, no matter what its function, is met at its opening by a sing-song burst of "Oh, that's so special!" or "Oh, that's so cute!" or the very worse "Oh, that's so precious!" Such language is known to cause diabetic shock in males. Once, just once, I voluntarily went to a baby shower, expecting only free cake. After ten minutes of "Oh, that's so special, cute, precious, etc.," I had heard so much sugar that the cake was starting to taste like lemons. I finally skulked out and have not been to a baby shower since.

The pain tolerance differential between males and females is occasionally exasperated by insidious outside forces and the interpersonal reactions of immediate sentient humanoids, which translated from TMS medical terms, means that getting hurt doing something dumb is made much worse when a female laughs at you. My father found this out the hard way once while fixing a tornado-damaged fence with his usual rugged work crew, consisting of my quiet, petite mother and me, then down to the use of one arm due to an injury. The tornado that struck our farm was the worse in our memories, flattening about a mile of fence, raining debris down on our wheatfield, and most tragically killing several of our neighbors. With the grim evidence all around us, we set out that warm and muggy spring day to begin the repair work, righting the woven wire fence and tightening it up to prevent cattle from escaping the fields. The twister had laid out the fence flat and straight, with no significant breaks. With just some minor clearing, the fence was soon ready to be stretched and secured to a concrete corner post. For this job, my father had brought along an old but functional stretcher system including a come-along powered by a ten-foot-long, forty-pound pipe and a wooden clamp consisting of two boards that we bolted along the height of the fence. By slipping the pipe into the come-along and attaching a hook to the clamp, we could exert enough force to tighten a quarter-mile of heavy woven wire fence. With my injury, I was unable to maneuver the pipe in place but could still provide a good push, so my father manned the position closest to the stretcher mechanism. My mother did not have the brute strength for either job, so she left it to us brutes. We were making good progress on the operation until the pipe slipped out of its slot, falling directly on my father's toe. My father had a pretty high tolerance for pain, but he could not hide the results of a forty-pound steel pole hammering his toe. Hopping around, his teeth gritted in a soundless effort to subdue a scream or colorful word, the silence was suddenly broken by my mother's high-pitched laughter. The scene of a one-legged man and his one-armed son trying to run a farm had overcome her reserved nature and she unleashed a gasping laughter that bent her up and down in hysterical convulsions, sort of like an insane Lamaze instructor. Stunned with pain and the sounds of laughter at his misfortune, my father angrily looked at his not-so-compassionate wife, tears running down her face as she continued to cackle.

His anger, though, was no match for my mother's infectious laughter, and his mouth tried to curl up into a smile but could not due to his still gritted teeth. Caught between screaming in pain, growling in anger, and howling with laughter, my father could not make a sound and just stood there, his eyes watering with one or more of the emotions he was trying to suppress. Initially horrified by the sight of my injured father and apparently insane mother, I finally joined along in her laughter. To this day, I am not sure if my father appreciated my contribution, because I ended up finishing the fence alone, though after at least I could use both arms.

The story of the crippled fence crew and the hysterical mother remains a favorite humorous story of mine, but another is more meaningful. Many years later, my father suffered from the debilitating effects of dementia. My strong, intelligent, confident father became a shell of his former self, his once steady, bright eyes now darting around like those of a frightened animal. Through it all, my mother cared for him, always at his side during the worst of times. During one of his many hospitalizations, he was extremely anxious, his mind wandering to somewhere dark and scary while my mother held his hand. Looking directly at him, her soft voice belaying her power, she whispered, "I will always be with you, promise, promise." She was faithful to this vow, caring for all his needs till he passed away peacefully at their home, the place he had been born and the place where he then died.

TMS and Communication

The great detectives such as Sherlock Holmes or Charlie Chan were always portrayed as having great powers of observation. They were aware of any little slip up by the criminal and could catch the most minute piece of self-incrimination. These detectives were, of course, fictional characters, because there are no such males with such deductive powers. Males are notoriously oblivious to their surroundings unless it involves the sighting of a female, and are totally unaware of the subtleties of conversation, most especially of the female kind. In-depth talks for a female are a cornucopia of family and neighborhood data, including complete genealogical, legal, and medical records along with psychological profiles and interactions. Male conversations cover sports, hunting, fishing, and food if they are hungry. Female interrogations with males on other topics yield nothing but frustration for both parties. A researcher friend of mine provided an example of this with a story of two brothers who talked on the phone for about an hour. When they hung up, the conversation with one of the husbands and his wife went something like this.

The wife asks, "What were you talking with your brother about?"

"Oh, nothing much," answers the unsuspecting husband.

"But, dear, wasn't your brother afraid he was going to be laid off?" asks the wife innocently.

"Oh yeah, he did get laid off," replies the confident husband.

"So, what happened?" she asks.

"He got laid off," comes his answer.

"Are they all right?" she persists.

"Yeah, they are fine," he concludes, thinking the conversation is over, but it is not over; the inquisition is just beginning.

"Did he find another job then?" asks she.

"Yeah, I think he said he did," says he.

"Well, how are they doing, then?" she asks.

He replies, now somewhat irritably, "I said they were fine."

"Emotionally, I mean," she retorts somewhat more irritably.

"Oh, I guess they are okay," the husband sheepishly replies as he gradually realizes that he might have missed something in the hour-long conversation with his brother.

The wife changes the subject and quickly confuses hubby by saying, "I guess they had their baby."

"Who?" the husband helplessly asks.

"Your brother and his wife!" exclaims the increasingly frustrated wife.

The TMS kicks into high gear as the husband asks, "They are expecting?"

"Probably not after eleven months!" answers the wife.

Determined to provide some pertinent information, the husband strains his memory and says, "Oh, yeah. I guess I did hear a baby crying in the background."

The provision of additional information only fans the flames as the wife asks, "Well, what is it?"

Befuddled already, the husband asks, "What is what?"

"The baby!" the wife exclaims incredulously.

"It is a baby," answers the husband directly, accurately, and totally uselessly.

"Is it a boy or a girl?" asks the wife as she begins to realize that she will get little information but much harassment mileage in this conversation.

"I don't know," replies the husband who also has begun to realize that he will give his wife little information but much harassment mileage in this conversation.

"You did not ask?" the wife asks, again incredulously.

"No," replies the beaten husband.

Sensing the kill, the wife again changes the subject. She asks, "How are your folks doing?"

"How would I know?" he asks.

"Because your brother lives next door to them," says she.

"So?" says he.

"So, didn't your brother say how they were doing?" she asks.

Finally, the husband has something to report as he proudly answers, "Dad caught a four-pound, six-ounce largemouth bass at Lake Keystone on a comet spinner using that rod and reel I gave him for Christmas when I was fifteen."

Speaking like a veteran with a fish firmly hooked, she patiently asks, "Fine, how about his surgery?"

Slightly confused, the husband stammers, "He had the fish stuffed!"

Still reeling him in, she corrects, "No, I was talking about your father's eye surgery."

Again, the husband is ready and answers with false patience, "Oh, he's fine. He has to wear sunglasses to fish now—the glare off the water hurts them a little, but my brother says he is driving the boat better now that he can see the buoys."

Stymied for the moment, she says with false pleasantness, "Thank you, Mister Lake Patrol. How is your mother's appendix?"

Feeling the hook, he blurts out, "My mother's what?"

She confidently continues, "Appendix. The last I heard she was having a little pain with it."

Suddenly brimming with confidence, the husband replies, "Oh, she had that removed."

"When?" asks she, slightly impressed with his fight.

"Two days ago, when it ruptured. Dad had to rush her in off the lake; she spoiled a good fishing trip, because the white bass were really running."

Panicked and concerned, she logically asks, "Is she all right?"

Now full of information, the husband replies, "I suppose so, she was not catching much anyway. Dad said she was moaning too much to get her pole in the water."

Now rattled at seeing her own fish slipping off the hook, she asks, "No, I mean is she all right with the operation? Is she still in the hospital? Is she okay? How bad is it?"

Now free and full of facts but no information, the husband says, "Honey, don't ask so many questions all at once. She must be fine. My brother said Dad was going to have a fish fry tomorrow for Mom's getting-out-of-the-hospital party. Sure hope she can cook it."

And so ends the inquisition with no clear winner in sight.

Communications between males and females, even with the best of efforts, can go awry without warning. A good, highly intelligent friend of mine once blurted out saying, "I do not want to have a good time; I want to find a wife." Although his intentions were honorable, the execution of his mouth was terrible. This points out a horrible symptom of TMS. The nicer the guy, the worse he is in communicating with females. My wife finds this truth when she asks me questions about my conversations with other people, because although I do not have anything to hide, I just do not get in-depth personal data on our friends' lives in thirty-second- to hour-long conversations. Contrary to her opinion, I normally do determine that my friends are still living, at least when I am talking to them. My personal research indicates TMS causes males to talk about inanimate objects rather than people, because that is simpler and less stressful. Males do talk and even argue about sports and politicians, but no real information is exchanged. Males' conversations tend to read like a hometown newspaper or a repair manual, being useful and practical. When males reverse the usual order of the universe and ask questions, females find them offensive and obtuse. The very prudent question of "Honey, how many miles has it been since the last oil change?" is considered an affront to a female's intelligence and is rarely answered civilly, despite what the car's warning light is signaling. Part of the understanding problem is that males wait about one second for the answer, and even then, the answer must be so loud that it could be heard over a jet engine; otherwise, the male's next question is "Huh, what did you say?" The only exceptions to this need for volume relate to questions involving sex and fishing, for reasons unknown to this researcher who has been snookered too often by the latter and will refrain from speaking about the former.

Despite all the bad news about TMS negative impacts on communication, there are treatments to combat some of the symptoms. One action is to often and sincerely say, "I love you." This should be directed at the male's significant female other and not to his favorite stuffed fishing trophy. Other treatments are to give standardized answers to all questions. When answering his significant female other, he should stick to fairly safe ways to respond to any comment by saying "Yes, dear." This works until his significant female other (SFO) thinks he is not listening, which he is not ninety-nine percent of the time, and sneaks in a trick question like, "Do you think I should buy all new furniture?" Of course, when she does buy the furniture, the male will bellow out his well-worn battle whine, "Why didn't you ask me?" and the yes-I-did-no-you-didn't debate is on. Some very clever wives with husbands of bad cases of TMS have been known to gather witnesses who are not believed and tape recordings, which, being male toys, are considered the gospel truth, much to his chagrin. The realization of being caught brings on a pout, which, if subtly and properly directed by the especially acute wife, can lead the male to mutter for hours, all the while hard at work on the yard. In some bad cases, whole flower beds have been prepared and planted before the husband realized what he has done.

In sharp contrast to males' conversations, females' communications are touchy, feeling talk about who hurt whom, or who is doing what, etc. These light, fluffy conversations include such drivel as how the kids are doing and how grandmother is adjusting to life without grandfather, or in other words, real life. Perhaps that is why women are the visitors to most patients in nursing homes; they can still visit with their loved ones even when their spouses cannot bear to go, because real conversations about loved ones are precious when your life is confined to a small nursing home room. The inhabitants of these sad places are dear souls whose lives are not their own anymore, and their dependence frightens many of their male relatives, leaving others to do one of the hardest and bravest things on earth, which is ensuring a loved one does not die alone.

Fortunately, communication symptoms of TMS often fade with age. It seems that later in life, grandfathers learn to speak of very important things in very important ways. Perhaps it is in his way of teaching his grandson to fish that a man passes on a passion for nature, or maybe it is in the way he lets his granddaughter steer while he drives down that old familiar country road that he teaches her independence. As he gently holds his spouse's shaking hands as she tries to feed herself in the nursing home, an older man no longer talks of inanimate objects. Then, his conversation is of life and is of the heart and from the heart.

Every so often, TMS may relax a little even for young males. My great-grandmother lived to be 106 years old, the last five spent in a nursing home. I tried to visit her every Sunday. I sometimes felt proud of myself because of how I loyally visited her, but these feelings disappeared every time I walked out that door because of her sad condition. I tried hard to make her laugh because I supposed laughter and her memories were about the only links to any real life that she had left, but Great-grandmother also gave back to me more than I ever gave to her. She showed by example how to live with grace in the most demeaning situation. She also taught me just how powerful a sense of humor could be, because our shared laughter was a timeless form of communication that we both could enjoy despite the circumstances. Even though she felt useless, she was still capable of the greatest service on earth—she could still show her love to another human being by laughing at all my bad jokes and smiling at my ridiculous teasing. In doing so, she made me a much more outgoing person, much different from the naturally shy boy I was before. Thank you, Great-grandma.

TMS and Aesthetics

Typical Male Syndrome causes males to act even more irrationally when they are faced with the unknown, which can mean about anything but definitely includes appreciation of items of aesthetical value. The army is a male-dominated society that often exhibits this symptom, notwithstanding its admiration of past weapons of destruction which it regularly displays as lawn ornaments. For example, one army organization within it that will remain nameless was housed in a five-story building with a nice view of a creek and wooded area; however, the military commander insisted that the Venetian blinds remain down in accordance with military regulations. The shades could be adjusted to let in light but could not be pulled up. The rationale, if you could call it that, was not to prevent the employees from wasting time staring out of the windows, which was done anyway while wondering about the commander's strange regulations, it was that raising and lowering the blinds would wear them out faster. Sooooo, this organization had these pretty views, permanently obstructed by the closed Venetian blinds, mimicking the effects of looking out at the free world from behind prison bars, which maybe was the point. One regulation concerning the blinds was not enforced, however. This one stated that the Venetian blinds had to be left at one angle, in response to World War II-era Axis spies signaling critical secrets like Venetian blind regulations from federal office buildings. It has been working well at this organization, because the Axis spies have failed to steal any management secrets such as Tootsie Roll safety steps, procedures allegedly put in place after one person stumbled on said candy, which hopefully was disposed of properly (eaten). Some researchers theorize the Soviet Union's spies were successful in stealing some of these government's management secrets, and after implementation in their country, they immediately collapsed.

Another subject area of TMS-induced confusion over aesthetics is the design of females' clothes. Most high fashion designers are males, which is a mystery beyond comprehension of multiple universes. The results are clothes never worn by anyone except female supermodels, male basketball professionals, and fictional crossbreeds of animals such as tiger-dolphins or ostrich-buffaloes. Based on how they look in those monstrosities, this explains why female supermodels are paid so much to endure such indignity. These clothes are too impractical to wear anyway. For instance, what is the purpose of high-heel shoes? It is an absolute fact (made-up statement) that a husband invented high-heel shoes and in revenge, his wife invented ties.

Art, especially modern art, is not appreciated by TMS-infected males nor by sane people of any gender. First of all, modern art is not art at all. One look and any male knows it. Abstract painting just means the paint bucket slipped. Metal sculptures are what bad welders do with all the steel they ruin. I once saw a bunch of old sheets hanging in a gallery, and figuring they were hiding something, I looked around them, not realizing the hanging rags were the exhibit and the waste of perfectly fine paint drop cloths. I felt sympathy for the "artist" who was obviously so broke he was down to selling his ragged bedding. Another exhibit was a bunch of stuffed canvas sacks, undoubtedly the work of an out-of-work feed salesman. Still another display at this gallery was a bunch of cardboard with paint spilled on it, apparently done during the painting of the men's bathroom. TMS researchers have studied this phenomenon to determine how busted construction material sells as art but could come away with no reasoning, only motive. The artists were thought to be devilishly clever con males trying to seduce females by talking with sensitivity about the art they spilled or steel they wrecked. Females are naturally thrown off guard by intelligent-sounding words coming from a male, and these ladies are convinced they have finally met a male not afflicted by TMS. Showered with praise and money, these con male artists find more sensitive and artsy words from female magazines, using said language to form near sentences, with the really smart ones avoiding all nouns. These males always refer to themselves in the third person, too, which is thought to be a way to disguise their real identity. Regardless of motive, the technique sounds intellectual and not self-centered despite the subject matter, which is all about their suffering for their art, while speaking from the back of their Mercedes. They also constantly refer to their pain as their inspiration, which seems to be true. One artist created his masterpiece by dropping his paint bucket on his toe, and thus "Raging Passion" was born. I wonder if my father ever made a sculpture called "Fallen Fence Stretcher Pole" based on the pain it caused his toe?

TMS and the Anti-Blonde Theory

Males often claim they are the more logical of the species, but TMS research indicates that is not exactly correct. Males often use crisp, confident, and totally wrong arguments to support their causes, while females on the other hand exhibit self-doubt when trying to convince a male that the sun rises in the east. Why this argument would ensue in the first place is still a mystery, but males have had a history of navigation mistakes since Columbus tried to find India. These symptoms of TMS are called the anti-blonde effect, which has nothing to do with a persecution of blonde females, something males do by trying to date, or even worse, marry them. The anti-blonde theory is the opposite of how the stereotypical blonde female, a concept invented by a male living in his mother's basement or employed as a politician, actually acts. A stereotypical blonde female is portrayed as pretending to be dumb while actually being very smart. The anti-blonde symptom for males is to act smart (and loud) while being very dumb. Unlike the stereotypical blonde female, who can manipulate their pretense with hair coloring, all males are susceptible to this symptom regardless of hair color or lack thereof.

TMS and the Toilet Seat Battle

Many females may assume that the habit of leaving the toilet seat up in a coeducational setting, read husband at home, is a sign of Typical Male Syndrome. This is probably the case, but more complex interactions are at play here. For instance, the classic case involves a wife feeling nature's call at night. Being night, the house is dark. The wife has a compassionate thought, which is her first mistake. Females should never have compassion toward males at night lest it led to feeding infants, once again, at night. When nature calls and she feels empathy, she thinks, "I love my husband and would hate to disturb his sleep by turning on the bathroom light." Now, the husband is not an insomniac; he has been known to sleep through severe thunderstorms. In a documented court case involving barking dogs at night, one researcher who will remain anonymous was known as the neighbor who "slept like the dead" despite the presence of howling dogs right outside his bedroom window. Somehow, the wife is convinced a sliver of light may awaken her knight in Tigger-and-Pooh pajamas, so she attempts her business in the dark. At the point of no return, she discovers the toilet seat lid is up, and her only maneuver is what little boys call the cannonball. Her convoluted splash and non-convoluted screams of female invective do not arouse her once well-thought-of husband. Dripping wet and hopping mad, she tries to confront her semi-comatose husband. In this state, his reflexes serve him well as he instinctively mutters one "I am sorry, dear" to all accusations. Somewhat mollified, and hoping that deep and sincere communication has taken place, the wife gradually drifts off to sleep, thinking back occasionally to the frightful scene and imagining that somehow this could be a sign that the whole thing was her fault. She imagines that perhaps leaving the toilet seat up was his way of rebelling against...her cooking, her nagging, her mother, his mother, etc. She only sleeps when she realizes that her husband did say he was sorry, and he is always sincere, isn't he? The husband wakes up the next morning, refreshed and with no memory of what transpired that night. The wife is very attentive that morning to the husband, and he, though confused as to why, considers it a sign that she is feeling amorous, and so a romantic moment occurs, and the wife, eager to please her rebellious yet sensitive husband, ends up feeding another baby at night. This advances my theory that leaving the toilet seat up is a Pavlov-type trained response. Males leave the seat up, females fall in, and then males get amorous mates. And some researchers thought leaving the toilet seats up was just due to male forgetfulness.

TMS and Mistaken Emotions

Some female researchers believe males mask their true feelings and emotions, while their male counterparts claim the male emotions are actually easy to see and understand. Females see intelligence and subtlety as a male slowly settles into his chair after work. "What is he thinking?" she wonders, or "Is he angry at me?" or "Did something awful happen at work?" In ten minutes, his only thought has been, "Soft chair." His grimace brings panic to her mind as she agonizes over her sins, thinking, "He is angry at me; what have I done?" He has just passed gas and is disappointed the smell has dissipated so quickly. After a while, he drifts away, and she wonders why he is so distant and distracted while he's just looking for a hammer to fix his TV remote control container which he bought after losing the actual remote for the tenth time. The remote is not in the container, but he still feels the need to fix something, so he searches till he finds a hammer. She decides he needs space to get in touch with his feelings and leaves the room while he passes more gas and hits his thumb with the hammer. As his eyes water in pain, his wife re-enters, sees his tears, and embraces her sensitive husband. He, sensitive only to his throbbing thumb and suddenly amorous wife, enjoys the embrace and his Pavlov reflex to like hammers is again reinforced, despite the broken container.

TMS and Balding

Hair changes bring out another symptom of TMS—the hide-and-seek one. With each falling hair, a male will seek out remaining ones to comb over the growing bald spot. With males, hair quantity is the thing that matters, not quality. Balding males are the architects of one of the most amazing structures of nature, the comb-over-the-top hairdo, a woven masterpiece the envy of any spider. The composition and structural elements are simple yet complex, an explanation to rival that of a modern artist. The basic ingredient, the hair, is found only on the sides of the head and the strands are about two feet long. Both sides are combed up over the bald top and curled around and around, forming something like a crop circle, another mysterious item of worship. Some petroleum byproduct is typically applied in heavy doses to hold the twirled hair in place and to give off a fragrance that repels flies and professional hair stylists. Once so adorned, these males are ready to face the world, but, tragically, not a windy world. With one big gust, the hide-and-seek style becomes the wild hermit look, with twin, two-foot-long streams of greasy hair pouring back down their necks and backs with the bald top fully exposed. Attempts to push the hair back up create a mass vaguely similar to an eagle's nest in an oil tanker spill during a hurricane. Some female researchers have cruelly recommended balding males "hide" from the public until they "seek" a good hair stylist, but this scientist just recommends a barber.

I do not have this symptom at all. My hair is thick and loyal with few deserters. Some well-meaning but nearsighted loved ones have indicated that I do have some gray hairs, but this is incorrect. I only have a few off-blonde hairs. Editor's note: Have I mentioned that self-delusion is a symptom of TMS?

TMS and Mechanical Talents

As you can tell by my lack of writing skill, I am an engineer by trade. My degree was in agricultural engineering and, for good measure, I got a master's degree in civil engineering. To my friends and relatives, this makes me an expert at all things scientific and mechanical. In truth, I am not mechanical at all. I can fix some problems that I have faced, i.e., broken before, but I do not have intuitive knowledge of all things mechanical. For instance, I was once asked about boat motor problems. True, I do know something about river hydraulics, but that does not translate into knowing diddly about the hydraulic pump of a boat. Needless to say, my reputation as an engineer was not enhanced that day. Another time my engineering skills were called into question involved a simple oil change. Now, I do know how to change the oil in my car. I can even change the oil filter despite the fact that the owner's manual does not show simple things like where the oil filter is (obviously, car manual writers and computer software manual writers are related). Anyway, my mother and I (a mechanical dream team if there ever was one) were attempting to change oil in an unfamiliar pickup. When it came to refill the oil, I was not sure where it went in, but I knew I would figure it out. Meanwhile, my smart-alecky sister, who I doubt has ever changed the oil in any car, instantly surmised in all her mechanical knowledge that I could not change the oil in a truck, and so, once again my reputation was besmirched. I must point out that my usual partner in crime in most of my mechanical misadventures has been my mother, while my father, who was also an engineer, was very mechanically minded, worked in design for a tractor company, and could even decipher a manual, could not be found. He always had sound advice, but somehow the situation never fit his words of wisdom. For instance, when he and the manual called for a bearing replacement, they said a slight tap with a hammer would easily "pop" the bearing. After a few days of prying, beating, and, yes, "popping," I finally got the bearing off. My cousins, who regularly replaced these bearings, usually burned them off with acetylene torches. I hoped they also burned the manuals and took videos.

I can recount one instance in which I became a man in my mother's eyes. We were driving our family's pickup in heavy traffic and suddenly became aware of our tire becoming flat. I pulled into a parking lot and actually fixed the flat without any major problem. This success in the face of many witnesses, and the summertime heat, made me something of a miracle worker in my mother's eyes. Considering my actions in the next incident, that was some doing.

During a Christmas break during my early years of engineering school, I had my first experience in fire detection. My parents and I were asleep when I first started hearing this mysterious beep every few minutes. My mother also awoke, but strangely enough, my father was once again absent while sleeping soundly. We searched and finally discovered the beep was coming from our "fire" detector. Not knowing that our "fire" detector was really a "smoke" detector, I used my engineering judgment to conclude that the fire detector was malfunctioning and was detecting too much heat. To lower its temperature, I placed it in the refrigerator, but the crazy thing beeped on. To lower the temperature even more, I placed it in the freezer. At that point, I thought I had the situation in hand because the "beep" was sounding weaker, but whether this was because the detector was icing up or that the freezer door was insulated and mostly soundproof, I did not know. After many more minutes and pathetic beeps, I was becoming desperate enough to read the label on the detector, cleverly "discovering" the detector would beep intermittently when the battery got low, and hypothesizing scientifically that this was the problem. Suddenly energized by the amount of information on the labels, I removed the batteries according to the instructions and listened to no more beeps that night. Fortunately, my sister was married and out of the house and my father remained in bed so there was just one witness—my mother who loved me very much and did not care to embarrass me further. Of course, the fact that she did not know any more about smoke detectors than I did helped maintain her silence as a co-conspirator.

Through these instances of painful and embarrassing research, the existence of a phenomenon called Male Knowledge Transference Dysfunction has been established. This malady causes otherwise knowledgeable males (an oxymoron) to try to transfer their expertise in one field to another. An example of this is when a physicist with a PhD tries to fix his car. If he is lucky, he would just blow the engine, but if not, he might be the first human to orbit the Earth in a Ford. Another example would be to have a computer software engineer try to shoot a basketball, which would result in a 99.9932 percent chance of a lost basketball. Still another example would be a lawyer babysitting human children. He might end up eating the kids. Or losing them. While certainly suing the parents and the lost kids, if they are ever found. As of this writing, no cures for this dysfunction have been developed. And do not expect me to change the oil in your car, but if you want a smoke detector serviced....

TMS and Careers

When seeking careers, both genders are equally inept at selecting college majors that feature many opportunities to meet. Engineering is an example of this despite its being a fine profession that provides a good foundation for an in-demand career that is challenging and well-paying, but it is rather nerdy and has been known to make accounting exciting. In addition, the school of engineering is not populated by the fun-loving, socially active party crowd, or at least for not very long. Unlike such majors as political science, engineering actually requires study, which explains why bridges generally work and our government does not. Parties are generally rare, and when occurring, involve celebrations of the completions of school projects such as mechanical teaser boars that are used to replace the real things (true story). For some unknown reason, social interaction is often limited, for the students and not just the boars. More importantly to the overall success of the genders meeting, the ratio of males to females in engineering has been as lopsided as about nine to one, so finding an available female in class can be quite difficult for the male. For the female students, the ratio works in their favor, allowing them to be very choosy about the males they hang out with. Because engineering is so tough, the females are obviously smart and can instantly rule out dating about three-quarters of the male population, including all of the pre-law majors. Being seriously dedicated to their studies, they do not just pretend to play hard to get, which is the deadliest female lure of all, except for the political science majors who are used to rejection anyway, but these females actually are hard to get because they are always studying. As if they needed more advantages, the female engineering students benefit from the innate interest humans have in seeing rare sights. Being surrounded by nine males for every one of them makes them all seem exotic, and indeed, there is no documented case of an unattractive coed engineering student ever recorded in engineering logs. Of course, to engineering males, the ability to design a working motor is considered alluring so other males may take engineers' opinions about females with skepticism. In summary then (for those male political science majors who might be reading), females in engineering are smart, ambitious, inventive, pretty, and serious-minded while surrounded by a vast sea of single males studying for similar careers of significant earning potential. As an aside, this researcher strongly encourages females to enter this field or other like technical studies, because we all need the best minds working on our biggest problems.

Despite few females historically picking engineering as a major, males still go into this profession, which indicates to TMS researchers it is some type of nerd trap. Historically, there have been even worse examples of purposeful gender separation. Some entire universities, such as Texas A&M and the Citadel, were all-male for years, which begs the question, "Why would any male want to go there?" TMS researchers have asserted through detailed surveys most males would have preferred being the first male at an all-female school rather than attending an all-male one. When these universities finally figured out that females and males attract each other, they went coed, and their attendance soared. The Texas A&M Aggies enthusiastically embraced this integration and developed some great traditions for sporting events. The most popular is their tradition of kissing their date after each football score. Granted, this can be hazardous to the kicker who misses too many field goals and extra points, but the tradition equally rewards the quarterbacks with accurate arms. Unfortunately, the Aggies have traditionally been a conservative, defensive-minded team that does not score much. These low-scoring and usually close games result in so few kisses that the males actually get more interested in the game than in their dates. If some coach ever was wise enough to bring in a high-scoring offense, he could retire as the most popular man in Texas, with thousands of babies named for him. Unfortunately, Texas football is filled with coaching figures with names such as Noodlehead, Bubba, Billy

Bob Bob Billy, etc., but at least the kids with the strange names would have college-educated parents who would send them back to A&M where they would inevitably experience the joys of kissing on football Saturdays.

Certain occupations seem to bring out the worst in TMS. For instance, plumbing and I do not agree with each other, which is especially galling to me as a trained hydraulic engineer with a master's degree in civil engineering water resources, degrees totally unrelated to plumbing. Like my misadventure with the heat/smoke detector, this is an example of Male Knowledge Transference Dysfunction, but when a person studies and pays for two degrees, it is hard to accept that you still flub up the same stuff whose word is in your degrees. My research involved my kitchen faucet, which I foolishly tried to replace. It seemed like such a simple task. However, the fiends who actually design faucets do everything in their power to thwart the amateur repairmale. On said project, I found out there were approximately 103,801 different configurations of faucets per brand. Each configuration was incompatible with each other in exactly one way. This one anomaly was totally immune to conversion or bad language, pointing toward a deep dark conspiracy perpetrated by the plumbing industry. Either that or the industry is so racked by male designers who cannot communicate that they just keep coming out with new models so that no one actually has to fix the old ones. These faucet designers must also serve as inspiration to their counterparts in the world's computer software industry, especially in the composition of the installation manuals, which are incomprehensible in all thirty languages that are included. But back to my faucet. I tried three different types of faucets over a period of about two days before I found a compatible type. My next accomplishment was to break my rachet. Discovering this mishap, I threw said tool and almost broke a window. After much time spent straining and grunting underneath a very cramped and occasionally wet sink, I finally managed to mangle the faucet into place, but the device remained possessed for the rest of its existence. Random locations of the handle would bring gushes of water, while others would bring only a trickle. The sprayer was apparently possessed by the god of water faucets—the evil Plumb Bob. Only after a worthy sacrifice and the utterance of certain connotations would the device work. The faucet and sprayer continued to whine and moan until its untimely death at the young age of five. A professional plumber replaced it. Within a year, the evil Plumb Bob killed the new sprayer, and again I foolishly tried to replace it. By the time my wife finished my work, I was honestly wondering if I had had a heart attack. And the sprayer still leaked, so we moved.

Jeannine and the evil Plumb Bob must have made a secret pact sometime early in our marriage. She can still fix plumbing problems better and faster than anyone I know. She has fixed disposal problems in mere seconds. True, she does cheat and reads the directions, but understanding written technical instructions is more difficult than translating hieroglyphics, so it still impresses me. About the only item that I can fix is the toilet. Here, males truly reign on a ceramic throne. Appeased by the sacrifices made at this unholy and unclean altar, the evil Plumb Bob leaves males undeterred in their home improvement projects there. I once successfully installed a new seat cover, using fire to burn one plastic screw off. Anything involving fire naturally brings out the pyromaniac in a male, so I was lucky the house did not burn down. I also fixed the toilet bowl, which required Jeannine's assistance to locate the cutoff valve just as I was about to flood the bathroom. I later even fixed a plugged line in our master bathroom. By the way, a male's shaving cream and a wife's long hair make a great water stop, but I digress. I still am unclear as to why my plumbing curse halts at the bathroom door, but I will certainly not look a gift horse in the water faucet.

Another new phenomenon involving TMS is the male dominance in communication technology. This may have something to do with the field of engineering (and other nerdy professions) being numerically dominated by males, but TMS research has revealed another possible cause. Anything that expands a male's ability to brag about something seems to naturally attract career interest. It is believed in some quarters that the internet and other communication applications were invented by males who wanted a larger captive audience. By providing an instantaneous method of bragging to the world, males have expanded the world of knowledge—their knowledge, or lack of it, along with associated efforts to correct their mistakes. Cable television is also a male invention as are most inventions that provide distracting amusement and the reduction of male work. The reduction of the work a female "traditionally" does is not affected by technology. Editor's note: "Traditional female" terminology seems to be affixed by stubborn males to tasks they cannot/will not do competently without whining so much as to make it is more bearable for females to just do it themselves. If someone develops a cure for this TMS symptom, a Nobel prize will be automatic. If something is invented that makes "traditional" female tasks easier, some male does something to reverse the progress, much like most office settings where the reward for good work is more work with the same recognition. For example, the invention of a mechanical washer and dryer meant that males just got more clothes dirtier. When females became "liberated," males took this to mean females got to do all the work at the office and at the home. It is notable that a baby birthing machine has not been invented and is the only known research subject that has not received a government grant. The invention of cable television also meant the rise of the sport of channel surfing. Males no longer watch just one show when they can watch twelve at ten-second intervals. If this just involved soap operas, they could go at six-month intervals and not miss anything, but for news programs, frequent channel surfing gets a little confusing. For instance, some males have become convinced through the television medium that the pope went seven for fifteen in the last World Series. Another confused idea born because of channel surfing is that the president smells like a spring garden when washed in cattle wormer. This theory on channel surfing concludes that it has its roots in the hunter-gatherer instincts of early man. Early man would hunt for sustenance and gather essentials. Modern man attempts to gather the remote and channel hunts for substance, neither of which is found without female intervention.

Blame Your Mother for Your TMS

In modern psychiatry and politics, which are both studies of deviant behavior, females seem to be blamed for all of society's problems. It is especially troubling that the ones who get particular blame are mothers. Consider, for example, teen pregnancy. Based on some male commentators, it appears young girls are running around everywhere getting spontaneously pregnant. Many people believe in immaculate conception, but most have doubts that it is the cause of a majority of teen pregnancies. Based on extensive research on new fathers, male researchers have developed a vague idea of where babies come from, although my personal theory involves water skiing as an aid, an idea that remains an outlier. From their research, these scientists have conceded that significant circumstantial evidence exists that implicates males equally in the cause of pregnancies. Mothers of all ages verify this evidence, but their testimony is considered obviously biased and would be summarily dismissed except the male researchers are too afraid of their mommies.

But surely, argues popular male science and superstition, females must be the cause of most of the world's ills. "Just look at the prison population," demand male acolytes before looking themselves at the numbers. "But consider how many wars females start," they counter before coming to maybe one if they count Helen of Troy causing the Greek-Trojan war by somehow seducing Paris into kidnapping her from her husband. They refuse to mention such English matriarchs such as Queen Victoria or Margaret Thatcher, whose propensity seemed to be more at finishing wars as victors rather than starting them. Popular, read male, culture must blame others for causing males to do such things as war, crime, home repairs, and other terrible things and who better to blame but dear ol' Mom. Yes, these researchers conclude, mothers are surely responsible for the actions of their adult sons, but mothers simply deserve better. It may just be a romantic notion, but women should be considered the nobler and more courageous of the two genders. Nobler, because they seem to seek the better things of life. More courageous, because they too often face and overcome what must be one of the greatest challenges in any person's life—the loss of their spouse. Mothers and wives, and women in general, are truly amazing.

TMS and Time Management

Typical Male Syndrome causes shifts in the space-time continuum (pardon the Star Trekese) in many circumstances. Ask any male shopping with a female for her clothes and he will say that time stands still. This applies to the husband with his wife of fifty years as well as the computer nerd out with his supermodel date. In the latter instance, time stands still for both. In sharp contrast to the pause in time that occurs while shopping in the women's department is a time warp jump that occurs when a male is shopping in the hardware or sporting goods department. In these locales, a male perceives two hours as a millisecond. The time warp especially occurs if he has a female reminding him of an impending dinner date with her parents in fifteen minutes. The time distortions are also apparent in other activities as well. For example, the movie *Gone with the Wind* lasts about one week when a male attempts to watch, but a round of golf, including the lies told afterward to the male's buddies, takes approximately ten minutes. Of course, the TMS-induced time shift may cause him to miss the annual spring cleaning of his 2,500-square-foot house, the push mowing of his one-acre yard by his ten-year-old son, or the thirteen-hour labor and birth of his daughter. A wife's fifteen-minute run for milk at the local convenience store takes an eternity for the husband if it means babysitting the aforementioned baby girl. The terms for these activities get a little distorted as well. The round of golf is a work productive "stress reliever," as if screaming and yelling about missing a two-foot putt relieves stress. The lies told afterwards are "establishing business contacts." The wife's labor is a privileged "bounding moment with her child," and the trip for groceries is considered a vacation from the children. A four-day fishing trip is a dedicated father's quest for food for his family, while the wife's part-time job is a relaxing break from the children. Based on these time distortions, it is difficult to believe that the world's population is still increasing and males are still a part of the equation.

When using the dreaded "r" word—relationship—males think in slightly shorter terms than females. Males think in minutes, and females in decades. The term "forever" means to males the time it takes to watch a "women's movie", while females seem to think forever means to death do us part, which might occur if the male complains too much when the father suddenly dies at the end of the movie. But forever should extend even beyond that. The memory of a deceased loved one is a precious gift; widows and widowers talk about their loved ones in very endearing and present tense terms. They talk about and even laugh over fond memories and reflections. This special love lasts beyond death, and while I always worried about my children and the dangers they would face in this life, I found comfort in knowing as much as I loved my children, God loves them more. The proof was that He gave up His Son. So, the love we share with our families will never die in heaven. Never and amen.

TMS and Philosophy

Females just do not understand philosophy like males. Males see the deeper, hidden meaning of life. For example, females cannot fathom the deep philosophical deepness of *Star Trek* and *Star Wars*. *Star Trek* researchers (fanboys) see the technological prophecies in the series that mirror the development of cell phones and other common electrical devices. The morality play scripts mixed with fantastic sci-fi plots are intellectual treasures that females fail to appreciate. *Star Wars* researchers (fanboys) point out the religious symbology mixed with classic swashbuckler action and sheer fun. Both genres use subtle humor to further complement the sheer depth of their genius. Male debates about the subjects are vigorous, though often high and squeaky due to puberty, but always deep, really deep, as in hold your nose in water deep. What unbiased philosopher could fail to comprehend the intricacies of the differences of the *Star Trek* original series versus the *Next Generation*? However, the debate turns ugly when the subject turns to comparisons between *Star Trek* and *Star Wars* and the ultimate question of which is better. Females dismiss this debate as the Great Nerd Civil War, but this intellectual struggle is one that cannot be ignored from its profound philosophical meaning. The question of who wins the fight between the Death Star and the Enterprise, an intergenre collision between a menacing planet-killing mechanical monster versus a mobile, fast-fighting, photon torpedo-firing fighting ship with a great historical name, somehow seems childish to undeep females. The breathtaking thought of a fight between a Jedi, a warrior priest with a colorful, menacing-sounding sword, and Mr. Spock, the logical, mind-melding Vulcan with a deadly grip is just too cool for female researchers. Fortunately, the debates, while heated, are not violent as the debaters usually cannot drive and are not allowed to walk long distances at night by their mothers or their wives of thirty years, and sometimes both.

TMS and the Submissive Male

There is much talk these days about the role of the "submissive" wife. Interestingly enough, most of the talk is from females. The amazing part is not that females are doing the talking; it is that males are not talking. When males are, they are even being smart enough to talk beyond the reach and whacking distance of their female loved ones. This raises the question that perhaps TMS is waning, but the answer is no, because it never does, according to the rising number of documented cases. Males are not talking about submissiveness because the whole subject evokes the image of kittens and most males like dogs. While it is true, a dog can be quite submissive, but that is considered obedience by males. Rolling over in front of its master is considered a playful act, not a submissive gesture to the alpha male of the pack. Another reason why males do not mention submissiveness is that it is so anti-John Wayne. The Duke was anything but submissive to the bad guys, and besides all that, the very word is so submissive that it hurts the TMS-infected ego just to say it. Another reason males do not talk about it is that females are. This could result in conversation, which is always a difficult and trying task for a male.

Now, for the record, I am for a wife being submissive to her husband. When I tell my wife to jump, she says "How high…are you?" This arrangement creates harmony in the household as each know their role. The husband should do exactly what the wife tells him to and then she should submissively watch him do it, correcting him only when life and property are endangered. In reality, the role of the husband as head of the family is not so much about control as responsibility. This role could easily fit the title as the submissive husband who first of all submits to God. He submits his life to the responsible care of his family, the primary role of a "real" man. My father was an example of one. He was a strong yet quiet man, protective of us throughout all his days. Decisions such as career moves and other major issues were based on what was best for the family. My mother, also quiet and strong, was a vital partner in every important action. From a financial standpoint, she was probably the lead, as for decades she kept my father on an allowance and handled all tax issues. Family safety was the one exception where my father took unilateral action. If for any reason he thought we might be imperiled, he led from the front. Whenever something was amiss near our family farm, he alone investigated. This is the type of submissiveness that is rarely recognized in the modern chorus of loud egos. There is a good yet archaic term for this type of man—gentleman. An equally good yet often scorned term describes my mother—lady. These terms are definitely out of fashion with those that associate them with weakness, yet history is filled with strong leaders who could be described by these terms. American presidents, no matter their parties, have always been clearly of a different class than the authoritative dictators they opposed. Great Britain was capably led by several strong female queens, and former Prime Minister Margaret Thatcher was known as the "Iron Lady" for substantial reasons. Noise is not strength, and gentlemen and ladies should not be anachronisms.

Likewise, the phrase "love, honor, and obey" is not in fashion in marriage vows. With all the truth-in-advertising laws, it should be so that grooms really know where their place in life is. Although the Bible refers to males as the heads of the family, and this is widely abused by non-spiritual males, any notion of superiority by males should be squashed. It is a particularly sneaky trick by God to put the most irresponsible gender in positions of leadership as a means of teaching them responsibility. Perhaps God made males the heads of families because He knew they were too stubborn to willingly follow sensible, straightforward commands without the guidance of wives who can control their husbands with just the simplest psychology. To achieve family harmony, males are fooled into thinking they are in charge, so they stick around to help females raise the kids while secretly being manipulated into acting like adult human beings. Males respond well to such an arrangement and do exhibit particular skill and enthusiasm in matters of heavy importance such as moving furniture for baby rooms. Once babies are born, the dads assume greater responsibility, like diaper duty and midnight runs for diarrhea medicine. With such a setup, family harmony is found, though it is sometimes a little messy and drowsy.

A woman's place is in the home. I truly believe this. I truly am glad I am not in a meeting of the National Organization of Women right now as well. I also believe a man's place is in the home because children need to be with both loving parents as much as possible. My wife Jeannine had planned on working outside the home for two or three days a week after our son Cole was born; however, she was miserable when the time came for her to return to her money-paying job. After a few months, she told me she wanted to quit, and I regret to say I did not want her to stay at home because of my concern with money. This also ties into a family's spiritual leadership and, in this example, the lack thereof. I was not cognizant of my family's well-being, but fortunately, my wife was persistent and I was not a persistent idiot this time. After about a week, I realized she was right. My wife did not use fancy arguments or persuasion; she just brought it up once more, and by then, God had been well on His way of straightening me out. He did His thing by placing in my mind the thought of who will be around my son all day, and it simply broke my stubborn heart to think of strangers raising our son. My wife stayed home with our children and we were all better off with that arrangement. We found that our evenings together seemed less hectic and more centered on family life, and our finances were also not adversely affected. We did not have to find and pay a daycare, and my wife was immediately successful in starting her business from the home. The little time she spent at clients' offices was easily covered by relatives or Daddy, a situation much to my liking. This man's place has always been in the home.

I work for the federal government (govamint in Okie English). As any (honest) civil servant can attest to, a person does not get rich working for the government but generally has a stable job that allows time with the family. I wish I could spend all my time at home, but my salary does not do much more than pay the bills. My dream job is to be the male figurehead CEO of my wife's company. I would "pitch the company" to male clients by taking them golfing and fishing. I would do most of the family's babysitting while pitching away because I plan on inventing the "family man's" golf cart, safely equipped with multiple child car seats, a microwave for warming bottles and kids' meals, and a DVD player for cartoons and golf videos, whichever is funnier. The "family man's" fishing boat would be similarly equipped. The point of all this delusional thoughts, occasionally I do have one, is that a father's place is at home or with the family as much as possible, and that may mean giving up certain activities such as drinking with the buddies, golfing, fishing, hunting, etc. The family is simply too important to neglect. The theory about quality time being more important than quantity time is bunk, because children have off-the-wall questions at unscheduled, off-peak times. They get also sick at the worst times and fall down without regard for deadlines, crying for Mommy or Daddy because only they can make it better. They catch their first fish or win their big contest when no one else would expect it, because quality time occurs when enough quantity time is spent for it to happen.

Memory, TMS, and Something Else

Another sign of TMS is memory loss, especially concerning personal performance, which for the non-deviant-minded includes most popular sports. Males tend to remember about four-hundred-yard golf shots hit in their youth on courses that county records indicate had not been built yet. They can recall in vivid detail that great touchdown drive they led to win the state championship, yet their yearbook indicated the team finished 3-8 and the males in question were water boys. A wise theorist named this symptom "The Older I Get, The Better I Was" syndrome. Fortunately, this researcher's personal memory has yet to be affected. My basketball career at good old Bixby High School was brilliant. My basketball scoring average was exactly 48.9723 points including 7.73421 dunks per game. We won the state championship in a thrilling double-overtime game when I scored sixty points, collected thirty-three rebounds, and hit the winning shot with Lebron James, Michael Jordan, and Wilt Chamberlain trying in vain to guard me. It remains a mystery why the state's official records do not mention any championships for Bixby in basketball and my buddies seem to recall I averaged about four points a game in my career, while they all averaged forty—all four of them, an obvious sign that TMS has affected them.

For the deviant-minded, the memory loss symptom may also refer to more adult relations. Males tend to remember coke dates as wild trysts and the tales told in boys locker rooms are only matched in delusionary splendor by tales told in the office by their fathers about their golf scores. This researcher has recently encountered a mutation in TMS, occurring about the time these males' daughters become teenagers, which causes abrupt modesty and honesty in the stories with adult themes. The coke date becomes an innocent first date with their mother and any physical contact is confined to the second date where Mom beat Dad in tennis, the only time Dad objects to the accuracy of the conversation. Here, Mom may interject some adult perspective by saying things like "Dad was always a great kisser," a statement which instantly provokes a chorus of yucks from the children and an embarrassed blush from middle-aged Dad. In a strange twist of science denial, the offspring of the human species all seem to believe they were immaculately conceived, reacting to any other argument with violent rubs to the eyes and ears in order to erase all visual and audible cues to the biological certainly of the unimaginable. Fortunately, with the passage of much time, all of these TMS symptoms fade, and by the time males are grandfathers, the wild tales become whimsical, jokingly told as if about another person in another life.

Researchers have discovered that a male's memory brain space begins decreasing at birth. Since they cannot remember this personally, the theory seems akin to modern art in that a subject described in big words by males dressed in fancy rags must be so intrinsically obvious that it must be true as well as special, elite, unique, and expensive to possess. My research on this subject seems to have gotten lost and I forgot what it was, but my latest excuse/theory is this memory loss is caused by the hormone testosterone, the chemical widely thought to cause TMS outright. It is my deduction that if testosterone were placed in a petri dish with male brain cells, the cells would instantly begin to clump up in huddles and then line up and bash each other. The resultant mayhem would leave many casualties and overall diminished mental awareness. The surviving cells would then eject tiny saliva streams while small arm-like projections would slap other cells' backsides. I would also observe that the introduction of a female brain cell would bring these activities to a complete halt with many male cells simply becoming disoriented and dysfunctional. Others would attempt to capture the females' attention, resulting in a massive pileup of male brain cells with certain death for many and extreme damage to all. Repeated exposure to female brain cells thus explains why males tend to lose their memories as they get older. I am not yet affected by this symptom, for reasons I currently do not remember.

TMS also affects the memory of the conception of children. No, it very rarely affects the memory of how they are conceived, just the circumstances surrounding the event. For instance, it is well documented that the birthrate in Nebraska increases dramatically after a college football bowl win by the Nebraska Cornhusker team. I claim that my son Cole was conceived after a particularly good day of water skiing. Both of the above statements are probably false, which certainly will not prevent me from presenting than as the gospel truth despite having no facts to justify them. Then again, if males only spoke their opinions when they knew all the facts, this world would be a pretty quiet place. Now, back to the circumstances of conception. A baby is never conceived at home unless after the aforementioned bowl win. According to males, babies are often conceived while on vacations or at least road trips. If the vacation is near an ocean, it happened at the beach. If the trip was to the mountains, it occurred in a log cabin beside a roaring fireplace on a bearskin rug—the kind with the head still attached (and a grizzly bear's head at that). For some biological reason, females know the circumstances much better. They can generally figure out the time and date very accurately but will not correct their husbands because they have enough problems dealing with the morning sickness. They are also discreet enough not to talk about it and even more so not to write about it. The gender divide transcends medical education because even male gynecologists have problems determining conception dates, numbering a pregnancy's length at forty weeks, starting two weeks before the egg and sperm's first (and only) date. This male math may explain why some females are hesitant to enter into STEM majors, because they simply do not get it. Other males see the logic as intrinsically obvious (magic) because males in white coats are really smart and expensive, so they must be right. (This does not explain how I won my bet with our male gynecologist about the gender of our third child, but with only a Coke on the line, I guess he just was not on his best form.) Regardless of the time and the circumstances, conception causes extreme shock for a male, resulting in an increase in forgetfulness and…some other things.

The Chronological Questions of Life

TMS also causes males some slight problems on answering "typical female questions." Some researchers add certain other adjectives in lieu of typical, but these terms remain unquoted due to professional cowardice. These questions are usually asked by family matriarchs who already scare younger males...and older ones, too. There is a logical hierarchy to these questions that are still incomprehensible to males. For example, immediately after puberty, Grandmother asks the young male the Great Question, which is "When are you going to get married?" This question does not necessarily confuse the male, but definitely annoys. After successfully answering the first by an officially witnessed "I do" ceremony, the young male, on arriving back from the honeymoon, is met with the "When are you going to have a baby?" question. This bewilders the TMS-afflicted male who assumes that one right response forever ends such questions. The male is so proud that he can give an acceptable answer to the first question that he is left speechless when trying to answer the second. This is a good thing for young females to consider. Ask a boyfriend or husband only one question at a time. Repeat the most important ones slowly and with little words. Lavishly praise him if he gets it right, a similar tactic when house training a dog. If there is a need for multiple questions, let him rest or eat a little so that his tired brain can rejuvenate. After a male is married and has a child, he becomes overconfident. He thinks there can be no other difficult questions from difficult females and cannot be shaken by his favorite great aunt Martha anymore. Then two months after his baby is born, she asks, "When are you going to have another?" Realizing he is beaten, all he can muster in response is a raspy stutter. Fortunately, the chronology is less painful in later times. After two kids, the question is a gentler "Are you going to have another child?" At this point, Grandma is satisfied with two grandchildren from her grandson and is starting to feel a little sorry for her granddaughter-in-law. After three children with the announcement that number four is on the way, the question is a worried, "Are you sure you know how this is happening?" At this point, the TMS-afflicted male is not sure himself and so no response is really expected. After four children, no more polite questions are asked. Additional birth announcements are met with an alarmed "Are you crazy?" which, of course, the male is by now. The fertile spouse of the male is revered as a "Pioneer Woman" and thus now gains equal status with any matriarch in the family. The male is now totally whipped and more concerned with his own questions like, "Where did all these kids come from?" and "How do I pay for all the college tuition?"

TMS and the Disgusting Stuff

Disgusting symptoms of TMS show up immediately in even tiny babies. Male babies cry louder but sleep more. This training serves them well, because they get used to giving orders without really working. Male babies also are more inquisitive. This is a pediatrician's way of saying, "I make more money on male babies because I am always sewing them up later." I wrote about this symptom with my baby boy Matthew on my lap. His interest in my wok caused o few problems in my Englush. This is another example of TMS at work in young babies. Girl babies do not sleep as much because they are worrying what boy babies might be thinking about them. They also cry more because they realize early on what they will be marrying.

Fad diets are always popular with most wives initially; however, they become quite disturbed when their husbands get on them. The reason is that most fad diets are invented by males and not females. Most of these diets involve eating lots of nuts, vegetables, beans, fruits, etc. However, no wife would ever support a diet that involves her husband eating more beans. If you do not know why this is the case, consider yourself very lucky.

TMS causes certain physiological problems in males that, although are not serious, are particularly disgusting to females. One involves bodily noises. Males not only make them, they perfect them. As little boys, males learn the fine art of making "toots," though not through a musical instrument. When gastronomically challenged, little boys burp, giggle, and then hopefully say,

"Excuse me." Men belch like foghorns, rub their potbellies, and say "That was a good one," to the applause of their children and chagrin of their wives. Males also seem to have a thing for scratching body parts rarely bitten by mosquitoes. This disgusting habit appears to be related to a male dog's habit of sniffing (I do not need to tell you where). Apparently, this was a learned response, from the owner to the dog. Another TMS trait is the sport of booger picking and flinging. A male believes that no one ever sees a booger being picked, but females can spot and be sickened by this from distances up to ten miles. The really disgusting part of this symptom of TMS is when males attempt to discard their prize. Males do not discreetly slip their boogers into wastebaskets; they blatantly fling them to the carpet, or even worse, eat them. The next physical reaction to this physiological disorder is the impulsive need to touch the person of the nearest female who has inevitably seen this display. Some researchers have hypothesized that this behavior is some sort of courting ritual but, if so, may very well result in the extinction of the species.

TMS and Sleeping Habits

Researchers have discovered a strong correlation between degree of TMS and sleeplessness. Basically, the more infected the male, the less sleep nearby females, and especially wives, get. This occurs for several reasons, the primary being that TMS induces males into an especially deep sleep during child-raising years, leaving Mom alone at night to worry about baby. Another reason is that males fall asleep faster because their minds unwind very quickly. One female researcher slanderously claimed that was because there was so little to unwind, but my research is inconclusive. Regardless, males do fall asleep quicker than females, with some claiming this is due to the formers' lesser levels of worry, with the causation again rather maliciously attributed to males giving females more to worry about. The effects increase with time, because as males age, they sleep even more while claiming to sleep less. Older males sleep about sixteen hours a day but not at one time. They typically rise about six A.M. and awaken their sleeping wives by asking what is for breakfast, which then consists of the cereal they find mysteriously in the same spot in the cabinets as it always is. Just after complaining about how little sleep they had the night before, they take a little nap which lasts from seven to nine. After that, they awake and do one chore around the house before taking an erratic wake-up drive for coffee with other curmudgeons. The drive itself serves as a wake-up for others in the local community as other drivers avoid the elderly Dale Earnhardts racing to reach the coffeehouse before their bladders give out. Getting home after solving the world's problems and causing the community's traffic ones, they eat lunch and then nap all afternoon. During supper, the wife wants to talk about her spouse's driving, so the husband naps some more. To have the strength to go to bed requires another nap, before nighttime finally comes and the male complains bitterly about not being sleepy. Seconds later, he is snoring, and after ten hours of blissful rest, he awakens to the belief that he is, once again, sleep-deprived.

TMS and the Holidays

TMS is especially prevalent around holidays. New Year's Eve is celebrated by males differently according to their ages. Boys long to see the New Year in, but their parents will not let them. Young adults go to parties and toast the New Year in with noisemakers and champagne, while fathers of young children are aroused out of their usual two-hour burst of sleep by their own little noisemakers and stumble around like they are drunk. Older males sleep right through New Year's like a drunk. Easter is a holiday that brings out the true conservative in males. Males hate waste and like to conserve natural resources like oily ragged shirts and any piece of meat or metal. This concern for thrifty living makes them somehow develop an incredible appetite for boiled Easter eggs. No matter how many eggs are dyed for Easter egg hunting, a male will want every egg to be eaten. Naturally, no one else will eat more than one per holiday. So, for a family of four that dyes three dozen eggs, that leaves thirty-three for the father to consume in about three days. The faithful family dog does earn points with his master by eating two or three, but even a dog has a limit of boiled eggs. Fortunately, the little ones break a few and lose a few (usually in the house) so the father generally only has about twenty-six to eat. Since the eggs go bad in about two days, he figures he has five days to eat them. As both husband and eggs get more and more ripe and ill-smelling, the wife usually intervenes and "uses" them in scrambled egg breakfasts and cakes and such. Of course, she actually uses fresh eggs and tosses the old ones away, but by this time, the husband is getting so sick and oxygen-deprived that he never realizes the switch even when he sees the fresh eggshells. The spiritual meaning of the holiday is well represented by the eating of the eggs as the children see the father rise from the dead to experience the joy of the Monday morning workweek.

Memorial Day is the next holiday filled with proud TMS-induced traditions. This day, typically considered the first day of summer, is a day to break out the barbeque grill and attempt to burn the house down. Since TMS causes pyromania, males from time to time simply must start a fire and females recognize this need to burn so they buy their man a grill to contain the damage and insure many trips for take-out food. Contrary to popular opinion, males' opinions at least, buying a grill for a man will not increase the amount of meals he will prepare; it is simply a way to minimize the smoke damage. A second tradition for Memorial Day is to take the family to the lake and go boating. Because this is usually the first outing of the year, it is also a tradition to have a boating disaster, usually starting when the boat will not, resulting in all the boating being done by a mechanic while the family wonders how long they will have to sit in the sun before they will actually feel water. Another fiasco that is common is to go boating minus the boat plug, resulting in an excursion of frantic bailing. To handle all the disasters, the lake patrol launches enough rescue boats to save the Titanic so that all the boats and TMS-infected owners have a tow. Of course, much of this could be avoided by pre-launch maintenance, but that requires preparatory thinking which comes from a portion of the brain rendered useless by TMS.

Independence Day means more independence from thought for TMS-stricken males. Nominally irrational males are freed from the relative safety of their occupationally hazardous desk duties, are actually allowed to handle explosives, and are again compelled by dark forces to light the old grill to cook with equally explosive materials. The simple presence of so much firepower overwhelms most male brain inhibitions and concludes in massive and legal pyromania. TMS truly causes males to have a natural attraction to flame just like moths. (Perhaps only male moths fly into flames; I am thinking government study money here.) Anyway, the normal urge to burn increases exponentially, which is male math for a bunch real quick. In a short time, males are occupying hundreds of burn centers around the nation while complaining that they just don't make firecrackers (small bombs) like they used to. It remains a mystery why organized fireworks displays are so popular, but some researchers have theorized there is a secret society of females organizing these events so their significant males and male offspring will not kill themselves. As for me, I appear to be one of the few males not affected by pyromania, because a few hundred pounds of fireworks (explosives) will last me a whole week. Strange, though, that I never have charcoal starter fluid around.

Labor Day is a great day of rest for males and lots of labor for females, reminding one researcher of a sort of national childbirth day. Sure, the males again attempt to burn down the backyard with the grill, but this "help" simply means dinner will be delayed until a professional, that is a female, handles it. Since Labor Day also marks the last day of summer, the TMS-afflicted male may try to go boating again. Fortunately for all other mariners, by this late in the season, boating has lost its novelty and regained its reputation as a means of wasting a pretty day on expensive boat repairs, so many males simply stay home with their fires.

The next great holiday is Thanksgiving, which means lots of stuffing, male stuffing. This is the day that males try to ingest an entire turkey by themselves and afterwards are too bloated to move off the sofa. The remote control was invented by a male right after Thanksgiving to solve this logistical problem. Females do not care much for Thanksgiving, because cooking a turkey for hours and then watching another turkey devour it in between a television time-out is just not much fun. Plus, with all the other male relatives unconscious on the coaches and easy chairs, there is no place to sit. They really do not need anywhere to sit because of all the cleaning there is to do, but with no males seemingly conscious enough to help, all furniture is occupied. Is it any wonder that the day after Thanksgiving is the busiest day at the mall?

Christmas is a male's favorite holiday. Not only does he get to eat and watch football, but he receives presents as well without having to actually give any, even for his wife, because after about the third Christmas wrench set, she is fully stocked and ready to properly train her husband to avoid shopping and just let her handle the gift-giving even for herself. The wise wife thus buys all the gifts and signs all the cards, including the one to her from her husband. She must be careful to not mix up the names, for then her son would never get his toys away from his father. This, too, illustrates the fun of Christmas for TMS-afflicted males, because Dad gets to play with junior's toys. This is important to remember if the wife is desperate and considers sending the father to do some Christmas shopping. Her two-year-old son could get a go-cart or a shotgun from Santa. Other challenges for using Dad as the gift shopper revolves around notions of what is a successful run to the store. In a male's mind, a successful shopping trip is to one store, Walmart, takes less than five minutes, and results in something, anything, being purchased. If the purchase is the intended gift, consider such a Christmas miracle. Wrapping a present is just considered a disguise to the male, with Christmas bags or even store bags sufficient, which makes the offer of store wrapping very attractive. If he is unusually industrious, he will write the name of the intended recipient directly on the wrapping paper.

Picking gifts for males for Christmas is easy. Just look at what the little boys are wanting for Christmas and get the same thing, only bigger. If your baby son likes to pound pegs with his plastic hammer, get your husband a hammer and a workbench. If your son likes to shoot baskets on his three-foot goal, get your husband a ten-foot goal and a leather basketball. A very wise and knowledgeable wife would get those adjustable goals that go down to eight-feet, which would allow a middle-aged male to dunk. In addition, a son that wants a scooter equals a husband who wants a motorcycle, and the desire for a toy Kentucky rifle for little Johnny becomes a passion for a black powder rifle for big John. Likewise, Cap guns become Colt 45s, and Tonka trucks are just smaller versions of Chevy pickups, all of which illustrate that shopping for grown males is really, really, easy but really, really expensive.

The TMS-stricken male always has difficulties in shopping for his wife, and the Christmas season offers no exceptions. The first challenge arises with pronouncing the stuff she wants. A male's total knowledge of female wardrobe is her shirt is called a blouse. Sizes are ludicrous to mention since they do not fit exactly with a male's, and he probably does not know any more than his own shoe and work glove size at any rate. Color selection is hopeless, because a male sees blue, dark blue, and light blue. A female would see Ocean Mist on a Clear Day, Naval Blooms at Midnight, and Well-Done Vegetable with Wine Sauce. Unfortunately, stores know females do most of the shopping and thus name their selections accordingly. Females love to get things called accessories. As a TMS researcher, I cannot elaborate as to what they are or even what they are an accessory to. In my research, an accessory is someone who helps out a crook, but why females like to help them is not clear, and no charges have ever been filed against a wardrobe accessory.

Despite the constant danger of infection, females very, very rarely get TMS, but for Christmas 2020, I saw a case up close and personal. My sister, bless her heart, is always searching for just the special gift for her loved ones. To help her non-musical family develop a taste for the finer arts, she once gave the gift of a very nice guitar, which sits unused to this day. Another year, she wisely encouraged us to donate to the Angel Tree, a non-profit agency providing gifts for underprivileged children, an act that was uplifting to us all. With her rather unique thinking, her gift-giving ideas are always met with eager anticipation, ample skepticism, and, often, loads of amusement. With that mindset, we were excited, of course, to learn of her latest idea for Christmas. She did not disappoint when she proudly announced that all of her children and mine were getting tasers. That's right; this would be the year Santa would be packing tasers in his sled.

My sister could tell by our shocked faces that she had some explaining to do. She reasoned that our children, now young adults and just starting careers in industry or college, needed protection from this dangerous world. Immediately, all males in the family agreed that any weapon was a great gift. True, my sons had that regrettable Christmas with their first pocketknives when they were both bleeding profusely before my wife and I were awake, but they healed well. Somehow discouraged by my wild enthusiasm, my sister turned to my wife for support but saw only panic. Trying to placate her best ally, my sister reasonably explained that tasers might prove helpful while hiking, jogging, or just walking around college campuses, which, incidentally, blindly forbid such useful things. My sons, though, required no further explanation and immediately announced they would be tasing the other. With three boys of her own who were like-minded, it was now my sister's time to panic, asking us, "They don't hurt, do they?"

Our replies were not helpful and barely coherent through our laughter. We reminded her tasers are used by law enforcement to subdue unruly and often violent subjects. Proof of their electrical power is easily found in publicly viewable demonstrations of their effects, showing grown police volunteers driven to the ground, shaking and convulsing uncontrollably. These examples are always discriminatory, showing only the one gender that would voluntarily subject themselves to such pain. For this same reason, young northern boys stick their tongues on a frozen steel pole on a dare, or here in the south, young males test the impacts of peeing on an electric cattle wire fence for fun. With these vivid examples in her head, my sister got her answer herself—yes, tasers hurt, and yes, they will be tried. And yeah, I want to test those tasers out myself.

Christmas 2020 at my sister's was pretty spectacular, with more voltage than the average Oklahoma thunderstorm. I do not know how Santa determined who was naughty and who was nice, but at our Christmas, enforcement was intense. Despite our soon-to-be rendered immobilized bodies, our family will gladly wish all readers, in the paraphrased words of Clement Clarke Moore, a "Merry Christmas to All and To All a Good" Shock.

Prehistoric TMS

TMS has been around since prehistoric times, but there have been some misconceptions on how the genders have changed since those early times. Most Hollywood movie producers, being male, represent prehistoric cavewomen like bikini-clad supermodels, but this is not accurate. During hard, short lives, these females looked more like T-Rex on a hungry day, but they evolved into beautiful creatures of high intelligence capable of incredible design and artistic creations. Cavemen were also dirty, smelly, and uncouth beasts, but failed to evolve and just obtained cooler means of transportation. Like their modern counterparts, prehistoric females also dressed the males, because those fellows just did not understand that zebra stripe and leopard spot furs clash as an ensemble, which could result in being eaten by a hungry predator such as a mother-in-law. In another blow to the theory of evolution, modern males still fail to pick out matching clothes ranging from baby diapers to Grandpa's sweaters. Present-day females continue the habit of dressing males, a trait first developed as little girls who learned to dress their Ken dolls and dads in five seconds flat. Olfactory senses remain primitive in the male species. While females can put on perfumes made from bat poo and still attract mates, males struggle to overcome BO with anything but the rankest of colognes, applied in large doses. Research is inconclusive but suggests male odor was indicative of his rank in the cave, with ties best settled with flatulence contests, events that seem to exclude females despite some misconceptions these were also sacred parts of mating rituals. As evidenced by the aroma inside of any high school male locker room, times have truly stood still in this smelly regard.

TMS and the Home

Males and females tend to have slight differences in home decorating ideas. Basically, females care and males do not. Unfortunately, males still express their opinions, much to the chagrin of females who are the only members of the species with any sense of good taste. Males like plain, off-white colors and mounted dead animals, probably killed by someone else and picked up at an estate sale of a male killed by the dust these trophies collect. Females tend to go for coordinating colors and fine art. Some items of interest, however, escape the understanding of enlightened male authors. For example, females love the latest craze. In the 1970s, females collected old milk bottles. These milk bottles were not the kind used by babies; these "collectibles" were the type used by dairies to ship milk to market. They were metal and could hold about twenty gallons of milk, and the rage then was all about collecting and painting these things. Males, being oversized pack rats, kept plenty of them around to collect, but did not exactly keep them in artificially controlled environments and instead stored them all over farms in leaky barns or outside areas. As a result, females were basically decorating old metal junk, much like modern artists. In the 1990s, indoor birdhouses were items that became popular among females. These typically looked like rotten bark homes for high fluting clucks. This brings up a related topic—the definition of junk. To a TMS-infected brain, junk is stuff that has no useful purpose, which for a male is a pretty small loop in the old lariat. Despite the narrow definition, wicker baskets, statues, stuffed toy animals for adults, and lawyers are examples of junk. To females, such useful items as scrap metal, assorted nuts and bolts, various unrelated auto parts, county fair prizes, and even John Wayne paraphernalia are considered junk. Females also do not appreciate mementos of their men's manliness, a subject that excludes their children. The non-living items in reference are mementos of a male's vitality and courage, badges of honor, easily recognized and revered by males and totally scorned by women. Such misunderstood treasures include such valuables as a third-place trophy for the church softball league. Won in dirt, that time-honored substance, most females would gleefully throw this manly award away. Other treasures easily scorned are the spoils of battle. Though not inclusive of official combat decorations, these war bounties recognize other less lethal but certainly harrowing experiences, resulting in the awarding of stuffed fish and mounted deer heads. To the uninitiated, these items are just dead animal parts filled with preservatives, but they actually represent something deep, really deep. These treasures remind a male when times were tough and a real man had to provide meat for his family, despite the presence of the ubiquitous McDonald's. The mementos are daily reminders of the game of life and death between man and a six-ounce perch, the struggle of a man and a gun versus a dangerous rabbit, and the battle to justify hours of goofing off when the yard needs work. Despite this incredible sentimental value, females still consider this stuff junk. The difference of opinion only causes problems when females attempt to discard these treasures in the guise of cleaning. Males would never throw out the female treasures, mainly because they either would never clean up, or if they did, they would use such items in their workshop. Expensive wicker baskets could hold greasy bolts; statues are made of good scrap material; and stuffed animals make great grease rags. When it comes to lawyers, well, even males would not mind throwing a few of those away.

Despite their overall superiority in decorating the home (and most other things not involving hurting each other), females fail spectacularly when it comes to recognizing certain fine art. One male researcher documented this evidence rather well when attempting to place a John Wayne picture in his home. (In a national embarrassment to our educational system, many uninformed citizens under the age of forty do not know that John Wayne was the greatest American actor of all time, specializing in western and war movies.) Apparently, females cannot see the depth and richness of the Duke (his nickname to the uneducated) in a backdrop of the old West. This enlightened yet outgunned (figuratively) researcher simply could not get his wife to let the picture hang over their bed (obvious first choice) nor above the living room mantel (acceptable second choice). Eventually, even the children's rooms were eliminated, thus limiting the entire family's hopes for obtaining true artistic appreciation and expression. Presently, this particular example of John Wayne fine art hangs in the garage where at least the wife has to look at him every time she parks. Maybe, just maybe, enlightenment will come, but the outcome does not look good.

In a home, there are male rooms and female rooms. The master bedroom is a misnomer, because the master of this room is the Mrs. No moose heads or other stuffed dead animals are allowed here, just lots of frilly lacy things and pictures of dead French-looking people. The wall colors of this room are named after flowers and space objects, though nothing in the script of *Star Wars* would be permitted. The master bath is the female's domain as well, although the male is encouraged to regularly bathe there. The other bedrooms take on the gender of the occupants. Little boys have distinctly male rooms and are decorated with such things as sports heroes, cowboys, and various earth-moving equipment, in other words, the same type of décor their fathers want. Little girls have rooms that look just like master bedrooms but with stuffed fake (never were alive) animals on a shelf. The guest bedrooms are female but are not so fancy that male guests are scared to mess them up. Organized closets are female closets; messy ones are male. Because they are rarely used for eating and decorated with fancy plates that never hold food, a formal dining area is definitely not male, while a den certainly is. In the wild, a den is a living area for animals such as wolves and is typically smelly, noisy, and chaotic. A den in a home is the same except that the four-legged animals are stuffed or artificial. The two-legged kind are generally rolling around the floor spilling pop and popcorn, and the kids sometimes make a mess there, too. A family room can be either female or male. If used formally and has clean carpet, it is female. If it has a regularly used television and chips are on the floor, it is much like a den and is thus male. The living room is typically disputed territory. The wife decorates it in all the latest styles, and the husband and children try to destroy them. This is where the five-hundred-dollar light fixtures get broken during the husband's golf practice or the kid's T-ball game. The living room is also where many a good football game was called due to Mom and her delicate house plants. The kitchen and normal eating areas are female rooms loved and adored by males for culinary reasons. Utility rooms are male rooms hated by females because the laundry machines (the only devices males never try to operate) are located there. Males use such rooms to store necessary home improvement equipment such as unmatched gloves and random bolts and nuts. Garages are male rooms filled with broken power tools and small tokens of their own distinct taste, or lack thereof, such as college-day posters, third-place softball trophies, and, of course, framed John Wayne pictures.

Since my wife picked out our house plans and most of the decor in our new house, most of the rooms in it are naturally female with a few exceptions. The master closet is also a safe room or tornado shelter with reinforced concrete walls and a reinforced concrete roof. With a steel door and three deadbolts in place, this is my baby, and I often touch it with fatherly affection. Being decorated in John Deere, our sons' room is also all male. The other bedrooms are a split. Painted in various colors I call pink and purple and filled with stuffed animal pillows, my daughter's room is most definitely female. The other bedroom is our playroom and is almost always messy—just like the males in our family and therefore must be considered male. The office is hard to identify. It has French doors, so its entrance is female, but it also has male characteristics such as a spare TV and few decorations. Since my wife uses it efficiently in legal commerce, the female characteristics are reinforced. Based on all this, this room must be considered bisexual. Our living room is like most typical living rooms and is disputed territory with my sons and me throwing balls against our ceiling fans while my wife has won the battle over my John Wayne picture which is banished to the garage, a disorganized mess of a space, a perfect reflection of me. The utility room also serves as a mud room with a steel sink in it. It is the place to go after a good day of tackle football to clean up or to place many of my tools and old work clothes. It even has a shelf specifically designed to hold baseball caps. Because of these additives, our utility room is male, despite the presence of the washing machine and dryer, devices that my sons and I have yet to master. Our porches house lots of toys and even some of my children's stuff, so they are male, which concludes the gender identification of the Henderson home.

TMS and Driving

Males and females react differently in traffic situations. When coming to a sudden stop, a female will always reach out her right arm, left in England, to "protect" her delicate passengers. This includes her 250-pound husband. Passengers in automobiles driven by males are out of luck. Males react to sudden stops by standing on the brakes, then speaking in strange and foreign tongues to the car in front of them. No one knows for sure what the intended message is, but it has been known to steam the windshield. Differences in hand signals appear to be based more on population density rather than TMS levels. In rural areas, many people drive one-handed, keeping the other one free for friendly waving at friends, neighbors, strangers, and various wildlife. In urban areas, hand signals are used to communicate…displeasure at the idiots who drive two miles per hour slower than themselves and rage at the maniacs who drive two miles per hour faster. TMS also affects the speed males drive their vehicles. For young, unmarried males, the disease causes them to drive much faster than average for no logical reason. Speed increases directly in relation to young females, crowds of adolescent males, and alcohol. This has been called the "knucklehead effect." Older, married males drive at varied speeds. When these males hear the words, "Honey, you need to drive fast," from their pregnant wives, they have been known to accelerate to the speed of light, with or without a vehicle. When driving their young children around, these males adhere to the posted speed limit. Their preferred choice of vehicle changes as well. Once, they liked low and fast sports cars, but when carrying their children around, they would choose mini-vans or Abrams tanks.

Conclusion of TMS

Despite its effects on all known sentient, humanoid lifeforms, a grouping that when liberally interpreted includes the non-female sub-species, Typical Male Syndrome remains a nearly serious problem of worldwide non-significance. While a United Nations-sponsored study would greatly help (the researchers), public officials remain purposefully unconversant of its dangers. At this point in time, a cure remains elusive, but symptoms can be relieved by drastic legal and/or criminal activity, or by a good sense of humor, which is currently recommended by male researchers who wish not to be the justified victims of said drastic legal and/or criminal activity. Fortunately, females, the actual sufferers of TMS, are overwhelmingly merciful and continue to greatly favor the sense of humor alternative. This truce, born of natural necessity, has held for centuries since the first caveman left a rock up on the first toilet, resulting in the first female royal splashdown. All research points to a continuation of the truce for as long as males are needed by females for, well, anything. Additional funding for intensive (editor's note: expensive) study is needed (for researchers' kids' college tuition) and will likely prove useless (except for the said college tuition). Females are urged to be cautious and compassionate when approaching the male sub-species and to use fried chicken or other foodstuffs when necessary to tame the beasts or at least cause them to overeat and then need a nap. My research has concluded that with luck and love, both genders can survive outbreaks of this disease, and maybe, just maybe, smile and laugh their way to recovery.